To good friends Ruth and Steven

We've had lots of good times

Here's to many more years of
good friends and good times

Best regards

Ed Bryan

# IN THE WORDS OF
# ADAM SMITH

## The First Consumer Advocate

# IN THE WORDS OF ADAM SMITH

## The First Consumer Advocate

by
Edward W. Ryan

Professor of Economics
Manhattanville College
Purchase, New York

Forward by William E. Simon
Former Secretary of
The United States Treasury

Thomas Horton and Daughters
26662 S. New Town Drive
Sun Lakes, Arizona 85248

Library of Congress Catalog Number 90-93270

ISBN 0-913878-48-0, Paperback
ISBN 0-913878-49-9, Hardcover

FOR MY DAUGHTERS, SARAH AND JENNIFER

# Table of Contents

# PREFACE

I first read "The Wealth of Nations" in its entirety many years ago for a course given by Joseph Spengler at Duke University. I still remember this distinguished professor noting that Adam Smith, unlike many other economists we had been studying, could "be read with pleasure over and over again." How true. For during my tenure as a professor of economics I frequently have referred to Smith's thoughts on various topics, have managed to reread his classic "with pleasure" more than once, and have learned that free markets offer more to the consumer than government planning.

The purpose of my work, the by-product of a wider research effort on economic freedom, is to bring this interpretation of the wisdom of Adam Smith—the father of modern economics—to those who might otherwise not have the time or inclination to tackle a nine hundred page volume. These include teachers, students, leaders in business, government, and labor, and in fact, any intelligent person interested in public policy.

My thanks go to Colette Hoey for typing the manuscript with professionalism and good humor, to Georgian Ryan for her suggestions and help with the proofreading, to James Millar who edited my work, and to Thomas Horton for his faith in this undertaking. Of course, any mistakes are my responsibility.

Adam Smith

# FOREWORD

President Bush framed his successful campaign for the nation's highest office around private initiative — "a thousand points of light." His immediate predecessor, running on a platform of limited government, was twice elected to the presidency by overwhelming margins. Failure of a state-directed economy in the Soviet Union and Eastern Europe has given birth to perestroika, the effects of which have reverberated throughout the world. Free markets have provided resuscitation for England, display unmistakable signs of life in Latin America, and until their tragic repression by a fearful communist government, had been warmly embraced by millions of Chinese. Without doubt, the decade of the 1980s marked a watershed in history when the tide turned in favor of liberty and free markets.

As we enter the 1990s, economic freedom will continue its advance around the world. Its ultimate victory, however, remains uncertain. In the face of a soaring public debt, the national government of the United States has failed to reduce its annual expenditures and an incredible assortment of programs, many with pious names but all calling for more controls and subsidies, are vigorously advanced every day. In this country and elsewhere, supporters of free markets must confront the forces of collectivist ideology, bureaucracy, and plain old vested interests.

For those who would emphasize the individual, and who seek a sophisticated discussion of the benefits of free enterprise, the wisdom of Adam Smith offers a most appropriate reference. His *Wealth of Nations*, written over two hundred years ago when government also dominated the economic scene, provides insight into such emotionally charged subjects as international trade, education, wage differentials, and taxation. But beyond these subjects, its explanation of the operation of free markets and the limitations of government reveals the close, indeed inextricable, relationship between economic progress and liberty.

"Consumption is the sole end and purpose of all production," wrote Adam Smith. This father of modern economics proposed a system which would coordinate a multiplicity of private decisions, thereby insuring the allocation of scarce resources to the production of what consumers value most highly. Moreover, the economic growth generated in this system would be shared by everyone, rich and poor alike. In essence, Adam Smith showed how freedom promotes both justice and prosperity.

Professor Ryan has performed a most important service with his clear presentation of Adam Smith's ideas. Not only has he selected wonderful quotations from the important parts of Smith's nine hundred page classic, but he has arranged them by topic for anyone wishing only to explore particular areas. Although this is a convenient reference volume, it should also be read completely to appreciate both the thoroughness of Smith's analysis and the grace and beauty of his prose. During a crucial period in world history, this is a book that deserves the attention of all who would understand and shape public policy.

William E. Simon

# CHAPTER 1

## INTRODUCTION

First there was paradise and in that state of bliss Adam and Eve had everything they desired. Then came the fiasco in paradise which was immediately followed by scarcity. This meant that no longer could all human wants be satisfied, and thus, the need to economize was born.

Economics is the study of how scarce resources — land, capital and labor — can best be allocated to satisfy human wants. Writing about economics can be traced to biblical times, and over the centuries philosophers, church fathers, statesmen and others have contributed their thoughts on various aspects of this field. But it was not until 1776 that a systematic and comprehensive treatment of economics became available. In that year, Adam Smith published his book, *An Inquiry Into The Nature and Causes Of The Wealth Of Nations*, (*The Wealth Of Nations*).[1] This was not a completely original work as Smith borrowed a number of ideas from his predecessors. However, he organized these ideas into a coherent body and was the first to show how an economy worked as a unified system. As such, he is justly called the father of modern economics.

Smith lived in the age of mercantilism, an era in which widespread government intervention in economic matters brought forth equally ubiquitous corruption, monopolistic privilege, and inefficiency. A good deal of *The Wealth of Nations* is devoted to attacking the government policies embodied in mercantilism. Sometimes Smith is depicted as a defender of big business and the status quo, but as we shall see, such characterizations are very inaccurate.

In order for there to be a consumer, there must be goods available for purchase. Also, it is important that these goods be supplied at competitive prices because with monopoly present, price tends to be higher and output of lower quality. Competition allows the consumer choice. Monopoly eliminates choice. Finally, it is vital that people have the income to buy products. Economic growth brings forth more goods and generates higher income.

Adam Smith showed how a nation could achieve a higher rate of growth. He was a staunch opponent of both private and public monopoly and, contrary to the tenets of mercantilism, believed that the benefits of growth could be and should be widely shared. He was a radical for his time and a true advocate for the consumer.

Although Smith was a product of the eighteenth century, many of the specific issues he addressed continue to be with us. Who are the beneficiaries of economic growth? What causes wage differences? Is international trade desirable? Should government ever subsidize this trade or erect barriers to prevent it? What are the legitimate functions of government? What characterizes a fair and efficient tax system? Does the size of the national debt matter? How best to finance education? These are a few of the questions with which he was concerned and for which he provided answers.

In undertaking this work the author had two objectives. One was to bring to the reader an understanding and appreciation of the wisdom of Adam Smith. Just as anyone who claims to be knowledgeable about English literature should be familiar with Shakespeare, so also the person who desires to understand economic progress and its relationship to freedom should acquaint himself with Smith. This is not to suggest that one need agree with all that he wrote. And yet, wherever one stands on the political spectrum, Smith's ideas are worth pondering.

The other objective was to allow the reader the pleasure of reading Smith's ideas in his own words. Adam Smith is easy to read and has a delightful way of expressing himself, as well might be expected from the man who taught literary style to the great biographer, James Boswell. And so in Chapters 4, 5, 6, 7, and 8, I have quoted extensively from Smith's work with relatively few of my own comments.

To provide the background for a more complete understanding of *The Wealth Of Nations*, Chapter 2 presents an explanation of mercantilism and Chapter 3 offers a biographical sketch of Smith. The final chapter assesses his work.

# CHAPTER 2

# MERCANTILISM

Mercantilism is a collection of ideas that dominated economic thought in Western Europe from the sixteenth century until the end of the eighteenth century in England and into the nineteenth century on the continent. It is a philosophy that is by no means dead, and many today find at least parts of it to be quite attractive.

Mercantilism developed at a time when the self-sufficient, feudal, agrarian economy of the middle ages was in decline. Gradually, commerce, money and merchants were becoming increasingly important. Nation states were being constructed in which people held a common allegiance and spoke a common language. A new world had been discovered and nations were determined to obtain colonies and spheres of influence. It was a period of intense nationalism, and political, military and economic hostility were widespread.

The goal of mercantilism was to build up the economic power of a nation and thereby enhance its military and economic prowess. Numerous writers, who today we call mercantilists, penned rather brief works in which they explained how a national economy might be strengthened. These pamphleteers came from a variety of backgrounds, but often they were merchants, administrators or statesmen rather than philosophers. Although not always in agreement, many of their ideas were put into practice. The actual policies of mercantilism varied from country to country and it is important to understand their basic features.

Gold and silver were of prime importance to mercantilists and many of them believed that the total value of these metals which a nation possessed was an accurate indicator of its wealth. Of course, today we have different and better concepts of national well-being but mercantilists stressed the precious metals for several reasons.[1]

On the domestic scene, they served as a medium of exchange in a period of expanding commercial activities. Also, they could be used to finance the construction of ports, canals, roads and palaces along with other grandiose projects that were part of the glory of these emerging nations. The international monetary system was not as yet very well developed, so gold and silver were acceptable in the settlement of trade balances. Last, although by no means least, the precious metals could be used to pay for professional military forces and to equip them with food, uniforms, arms, ships and the other accoutrements of war — and if nothing else, these nations went to war.

To obtain the gold and silver, mercantilists believed that government should play an important role as a regulator and director of economic activity. Although government certainly had injected itself into the medieval economy, the role of the state during mercantilism became much more centralized and extensive.

Mercantilists wanted to export a greater value of goods to foreign nations than were imported. If this policy met with success, foreign nations would settle their deficits by paying gold and silver. In order to realize this end, nations sought to discourage imports and stimulate exports.

To the extent possible, products consumed in a nation should be produced at home. Subsidies and tariff protection were awarded to industries that otherwise might falter under the pressure of international competition. Ideally, imports were to be restricted to raw materials which then would be worked up into finished products and sold to colonies or to other countries.

Nations went to great lengths to stimulate industry. Monopoly privileges were awarded to inventors as well as to others who simply were politically well connected. The immigration of skilled artisans was encouraged and their emigration prohibited. To stimulate export industries, subsidies were given and regulations were promulgated to insure that merchandise would be of high quality. So anxious were mercantilists to acquire gold and silver that sometimes they permitted goods to be sold to the very nations with which they were at war as long as payment was in hard money. The state awarded monopolies to companies undertaking commercial activities in other parts of the world and such companies, like the East India Company, were placed under government supervision.

England discouraged the consumption of sugar and tea because these products had to be imported. That nation offered subsidies to numerous industries including mining, armaments, coal, glass, vinegar and leather. The importation of calico was prohibited in order to stimulate the wool industry. In fact, at the behest of that industry, the deceased were required to be buried in shrouds made of wool, and the export of live sheep was forbidden. Moreover, this Protestant country required people to refrain from eating meat twice a week. This was intended to stimulate the fishing industry, for in those days fishing vessels and their sailors were used by the navy during time of war.

Mercantilism was practiced most vigorously in France. Here also, certain industries were subsidized and monopolistic privileges awarded to foster their development. To insure uniform product quality, the state laid down regulations for all parts of the production process. In the manufacture of cloth, for instance, hundreds of pages of rules specified the type of dye as well as the number, width and quality of threads that must be used. The number of towns allowed to manufacture a particular product was limited. The state decided what was to be produced, how it was to be produced, who would perform the work, where it was to be accomplished, what wages could be received, and what prices must be charged.

Colonies were an integral component of mercantilist planning and were established primarily for economic reasons. One of their functions was to develop raw materials which would be made into finished products by the mother country. They also served as markets for its exports. So as not to compete with domestic producers, the colonists were limited in what they could manufacture, and the transportation of most goods was restricted to the vessels of the home nation. In England, laws collectively known as the Navigation Acts were designed to implement these ideas during the seventeenth century.

Labor policy, another aspect of mercantile thought, contained several parts. First, a large population was favored as this would insure an adequately sized labor force to produce goods for export and also provide soldiers and sailors for military adventures. In France, population growth was encouraged with tax concessions for early marriage and tax exemptions for families with ten or more children. (Children who had died in the military were counted while those who entered the clergy were not.)

Second, the state concerned itself with allocating people to different occupations as well as fixing their wages. In England, the famous Statute of Artificers of 1563 established a detailed code for the regulation of labor. Because government took upon itself the responsibility of insuring an adequate food supply, able-bodied men, unless exempt by reason of guild membership or social status, were forced to work in agriculture. These farm laborers were placed under contract for a year and both the employer and the employee could be penalized if the agreement was violated. For an adequate supply of skilled labor to be available, young boys were apprenticed to various trades. Maximum and minimum wages as well as hours of work were established by local authorities who were ultimately responsible to the crown.

Although labor policy was not deliberately designed to impoverish the work force, it was believed that if wages rose too high, idleness and dissipation surely would ensue. And so, mercantilists advocated low wages and continuous employment. With such a policy, the nation's commerce, especially the international sector, would not be harmed, and the upper classes could continue to maintain their standard of living. The prose of two writers in this era, William Temple and Arthur Young, provide rather vivid evidence of this point of view.

When these children are four years old, they shall be sent to the country work-house and there be taught to read two hours a day, and be kept full employed the rest of their time, in any of the manufactures of the house, which best suits their age, strength and capacity. If it should be objected that, at these early years, they cannot be made useful, I reply, that at four years of age, there are sturdy employments in which children can earn their living; but besides that, there is a very considerable use in their being, somehow or other constantly employed, at least, twelve hours a day, whether they earn their living or not; for by these means, we hope that the rising generation will be so habituated to constant employment that it would, at length prove agreeable and entertaining to them.[2]

Every one but an ideot [sic] knows that the lower classes must be kept poor or they will never be industrious. I do not mean, that the poor in England are to be kept like the poor of France, but, the state of the country considered they must be (like all mankind) in poverty, or they will not work.[3]

The final component of national labor policy focused upon the poor. In England, prior to the Protestant reformation, the Roman Catholic Church had been the cornerstone of the relief system. It encouraged the giving of alms and established monasteries to assist the unfortunate. However, during the reformation Church property had been confiscated and its ability to help the poor had markedly deteriorated. To further aggravate matters, an enclosure movement took place which had the effect of increasing the number of England's poor. This resulted from a rise in the demand for wool and landlords, hoping to obtain profits from this expanding market, enclosed their land so that sheep might graze. An important side effect of all this was to expel tenants from the land. And so, deprived of their traditional right to work the soil, many of them fell into poverty.

The system that then developed in mercantile England made poor relief a local responsibility. Taxes to support the poor were levied in each parish and local officials administered these funds. Those unable to work were taken care of or permitted to beg while those physically able received tasks to perform. Authorities were particularly concerned about the able-bodied who did not want to work and when these were found, they were beaten and sent to a house of correction.

Public policy also made it difficult for a poor person to improve his condition by moving to another area. The Law of Settlement allowed the town fathers to return a newly arrived person to the community from which he originated if he even looked like he might become a financial burden. It was a harsh system reflecting a popular belief (at least popular in the minds of the upper classes) that poverty was connected with vice and wealth with virtue.

Of course, this age, like others, was not without its accomplishments. Mercantilists were somewhat successful in removing or at least reducing local taxes on goods and numerous petty tolls that impeded the free movement of products within a nation. The development of uniform weights, measures and coins assisted the growth of economic activity. This era also witnessed the construction of roads, canals and bridges, as well as grandiose palaces, museums, and other public buildings which today are considered national treasures. The tempo of life picked up and, generally speaking, there was economic progress.

There also were serious problems. Mercantilists sought to achieve economic might through government planning and regulation, but much of this was unsuccessful. Monopolistic practices were fostered, inefficient business firms kept alive with government assistance, and innovation made difficult. An army of bureaucrats enforced the multiplicity of regulations that bound every industry and the system, enveloped in what today we call red tape, grew to be despised. Wages were depressed, the poor treated badly, and national rivalries inflamed. Adam Smith wrote his classic work toward the end of this period and was very much influenced by what he observed. Let us now turn to this fascinating man.

# CHAPTER 3

## ADAM SMITH

Adam Smith was born in 1723 in Kirkaldy, a small town near Edinburgh, Scotland. His father, a Judge Advocate for Scotland and a Comptroller of Customs, died just before his birth. He was taken care of by his mother, Margaret, whom he deeply loved, and except for his travels, he stayed with her until her death at age ninety. Smith never married.

Although frail in body, Adam Smith had a wonderful disposition and was very well liked. As a youngster, he developed a love of books and displayed a superb memory. The future father of economics was not without idiosyncrasy, for he often talked to himself and was notoriously absent-minded.

At the age of fourteen, Smith went off to the University of Glasgow. At that time, this institution was the scene of intellectual ferment and Smith had the opportunity, as had his friend in later life, David Hume, to study under Professor Francis Hutcheson. This teacher had a great influence on Smith, and it was he who developed the concept of liberty in the mind of his young pupil.

Smith had a successful career at Glasgow. He remained there until the age of seventeen whereupon he was awarded a scholarship to Balliol College at Oxford. However, with Scots discriminated against, teachers not inclined to do much teaching, and petty intrigue abundant, the stay at Oxford was not a happy one. It was such an intellectually stultifying atmosphere that he almost was expelled for reading Humes', *Treatise of Human Nature*. Nonetheless, the genial Adam Smith applied himself to his studies and spent much time in the library. He read widely but was especially interested in law, the classics, and belles lettres.

In 1746 he left Oxford and returned to Kirkaldy where he devoted himself to the composition of essays and fine literature. Two years later he was invited to give a series of public lectures in Edinburgh on the subjects of English literature and the philosophy of law. These were well attended and well received.

A vacancy occurred at Glasgow University in 1751 and this enabled Smith to be appointed Professor of Logic. In that role he lectured not only on logic, but also on rhetoric and belles lettres. Subsequently, he was awarded the Chair of Moral Philosophy and he lectured on a wide range of subjects, for in those days, moral philosophy encompassed theology, ethics, justice and political economy. Adam Smith was a successful and well-liked teacher. The ideas which he developed in the lectures on political economy eventually found their way into *The Wealth of Nations*, but it was the lectures on ethics that became the basis of his first book.

In *The Theory of Moral Sentiments*, first published in 1759, Smith conducted an investigation into the

ethics of human behavior and sought to determine
how moral principles are derived. He noted that
man is possessed by many motives, but believed
one of the strongest to be self-interest. This drive,
he felt, is held in check by ". . . reason, principle,
conscience, the inhabitant of the breast, the man
within, the great judge and arbiter of our conduct."[1]
In other words, it is through our conscience that
individuals obtain the guidance to pursue their own
interest without acting unethically, that is, in violation of God's rules. Smith's "third person" or "impartial spectator" does allow us to improve our
material welfare, but also requires that we balance
our behavior by avoiding harm to others and by
affording them generosity and kindness. Obedience
to the laws of the diety brings inner peace while
their violation elicits shame and discontent. It is in
this manner that natural harmony is promoted and
the well being of society served. The theme of natural harmony is repeated in *The Wealth of Nations*.

*The Theory of Moral Sentiments* was a huge success and went through six editions during Smith's
life. Delightfully written, it was considered important for its philosophical ideas. Smith became
widely known, his companionship was sought, and
the number of his students increased. James Boswell, later to become the famous biographer, en-
rolled in one of Smith's classes and received
instruction in literary style.

One of those who became enamoured with Smith's
work was Charles Townshend. This was the same

person who later served as Chancellor of the Exchequer and gained a degree of fame for his role in the tax on tea imported into the American colonies. Townshend was so taken with this book that he decided to engage Smith as a tutor for his stepson, the Duke of Buccleuch, and his offer of three hundred pounds a year for the rest of his life induced Smith to resign from Glasgow. Part of the new assignment included a foreign tour, and so in 1764 Smith and the young Duke journeyed to the continent.

He was warmly received in France as *The Theory of Moral Sentiments* had already accorded him international acclaim. Introductions to the important and influential people of that country were obtained and he even met several times with Voltaire. Smith also became acquainted with a group of economists known as Physiocrats, a school of economic thought which attempted to show how wealth circulated in the economy and how economic growth could be achieved through the encouragement of agriculture and free trade. Physiocracy, a reaction to the inefficiency, inequity and corruption of French mercantilism, also held that the economic role of government should be kept to a minimum, in other words, laissez-faire. It is impossible to know precisely how much these ideas affected Smith, although probably there was some influence.

Besides his conversations with the Physiocrats, Smith took a keen interest in the French economy. During this period he began work on *The Wealth of Nations*.

Adam Smith lived and died in the eighteenth century and what he observed helped to shape his ideas. In his time, the British economy primarily was agricultural, and manufacturing was dominated by textile production which often took place in the home. Some large-scale businesses were to be found in coal and iron, but the size of most firms was small. Factories, although not unknown, were not very important, nor were most tools especially complex. Part of the population lived in luxury, but the vast majority owned no land, held few possessions, and received low wages from employers who often treated them harshly.

Although England still was in the grasp of mercantilism, the tentacles of that system were loosening. Economic theory predicts that people will engage in an illegal activity if they expect that its benefits will exceed its costs. This happened in the eighteenth century. People took the initiative and found ways to circumvent state regulations. They entered trades without serving apprenticeships and violated guild rules when superior production methods were discovered. Clandestine voyages were undertaken to obtain a share in the monopoly profits of the chartered companies, and no small amount of smuggling took place. The comments of Wesley Mitchell on his own experiences are instructive.

This summer [1926] I happened to meet an Englishman whose family lived on the southern coast of England and who had

been a clergyman for a long while. He told
me that the church in which his family was
most interested was regularly used in the
days of mercantilism as a warehouse in
which smuggled brandies and French wines
were stored, and that frequently enough,
the Church services themselves were interrupted by the arrival of some messenger be-
longing to the smuggling gang who reported
a company of soldiers moving their way. The
whole congregation would be dispersed to
move the smuggled goods to a safe place.
That kind of thing was going on through all
classes of society.[2]

And so in spite of mercantilism, the English economy was expanding. Advancements in agricultural
technology allowed the support of a larger population. Roadways improved, the cost of shipping de-
clined, financial institutions developed, markets
widened, and the volume of exchange increased.
The rewards for initiative stimulated change and
growth while the liberal ideas of private property
and greater freedom for the individual in both the
economic and political arenas were taking hold.

Of course, the eighteenth century also is known
for its non-economic achievements and here too the
different art forms that developed were the result
of individual initiative. In music, Handel brought
forth the oratorio; the portrait was developed by
Gainsborough and Reynolds; literature took a new

form under the influence of Defoe, Richardson, and Fielding; Boswell set down a different sort of biography; and Addison and Steele changed the nature of journalism.[3]

We see that Adam Smith absorbed many influences, both economic and non-economic, in the books he read, and in his observations and conversations in Kirkaldy, Glasgow, Edinburgh and France. Let us now examine his masterpiece.

# CHAPTER 4

# ECONOMIC GROWTH

*The Wealth of Nations* was published on March 9, 1776. This large volume—over nine hundred pages in the Cannan edition—covers a multitude of topics including agriculture, domestic and international trade, manufacturing, the merchant, the producer, the worker, the government, money, public borrowing, taxes, the colonies, the opulence of the Saracen empire, the bounty on herring, and the rate of interest in China. Of course, we will not be concerned with every aspect of the work, but rather adopt a more narrow focus. This chapter examines Smith's perspective on wealth, human nature, and how competitive markets foster economic growth beneficial to the greater society. The next four chapters discuss the international economy, public policy, the proper role of government and Adam Smith as a consumer advocate. Each of these chapters present Smith's ideas in his own words under various topical headings.

## WEALTH, MONEY, AND THE PRECIOUS METALS

The full title of Smith's book, *An Inquiry Into The Nature and Causes of The Wealth of Nations*, accurately describes its essence. Unlike the mercantilists whose notion of national wealth focused upon gold and silver, Smith believed it consisted of real output, ". . . the annual produce of the land and labor of the society."[1], which he felt should be calculated on a per capita basis. The following comments illustrate his thoughts on money and the precious metals.

> Money is neither a material to work upon, nor a tool to work with; and though the wages of the workman are commonly paid to him in money, his real revenue, like that of all other men, consists, not in the money, but in the money's worth; not in the metal pieces, but in what can be got for them.[2]

> It would be too ridiculous to go about seriously to prove, that wealth does not consist in money, or in gold and silver; but in what money purchases, and is valuable only for purchasing.[3]

> It is not always necessary to accumulate gold and silver, in order to enable a country to carry on foreign wars, and to maintain

Adam Smith

fleets and armies in distant countries. Fleets and armies are maintained, not with gold and silver, but with consumable goods. The nation which, from the annual produce of its domestic industry, from the annual revenue arising out of its lands, labour, and consumable stock, has wherewithal to purchase those consumable goods in distant countries, can maintain foreign wars there.[4]

# HUMAN NATURE AND COMPETITIVE MARKETS

Smith also differs significantly from the mercantilists on how to make this real output grow — what today we refer to as economic development. There are several parts to Smith's development process but one of the most important is the operation of free competitive markets, so let us start with that.

Adam Smith was the first to explain in detail the role of human beings in the development of markets and how these markets function to solve the basic economic problems that confront any society: what goods to produce, how to produce them, and to whom should they be distributed.

Smith placed great emphasis on people in the growth process. He felt that they came equipped with, ". . . the propensity to truck, barter, and exchange one thing with another."[5] Moreover, this was unique to them for, "Nobody ever saw a dog make a fair and deliberate exchange of one bone for another with another dog."[6] He then goes on to state his case that self-interest is a dominant human motive.

> When an animal wants to obtain something either of a man or of another animal, it has no other means of persuasion but to gain the favour of those whose service it requires. A puppy fawns upon its dam, and a spaniel endeavours by a thousand attractions to engage

the attention of its master who is at dinner, when it wants to be fed by him. Man sometimes uses the same arts with his brethren, and when he has no other means of engaging them to act according to his inclinations, endeavours by every servile and fawning attention to obtain their good will. He has not time, however, to do this upon every occasion. In civilized society he stands at all times in need of the cooperation and assistance of great multitudes, while his whole life is scarce sufficient to gain the friendship of a few persons. In almost every other race of animals each individual, when it is grown up to maturity, is entirely independent, and in its natural state has occasion for the assistance of no other living creature. But man has almost constant occasion for the help of his brethren, and it is in vain for him to expect it from their benevolence only. He will be more likely to prevail if he can interest their self-love in his favour, and show them that it is for their own advantage to do for him what he requires of them. Whoever offers to another a bargain of any kind, proposes to do this. Give me that which I want, and you shall have this which you want, is the meaning of every such offer; and it is in this manner that we obtain from one another the far greater part of those good offices which we stand in need of . It is not from the benevolence of the butcher, the brewer, or the baker, that we expect our dinner, but from their regard to their own interest. We address ourselves, not to their humanity but to their self-love, and never talk to them of our own necessities but of their advantages.

A market exists when buyer and seller come together to effect an exchange. The emergence of prices is a vital part of the market system that Smith described. What he called the natural price is the lowest price at which a person would continue to sell a product over time. A commodity selling at such a price would bring in enough revenue to pay the average or natural wage and rent and still yield a profit. In addition to the natural price, there also is a market price which is the actual price at which the product sells. The actual market price may be greater or less than its natural price. However, when this occurs competitive forces will push the two toward equality. Let us see how.

If people want more of one product and less of another product their wishes will be carried out within the framework of markets. The market price of the product that is in greater demand will be bid up and, thereby, rise above its natural level and yield larger profits. In contrast, the price of the commodity for which demand has fallen will drop below its natural level and profits will diminish. In response to these signals, businessmen will leave the declining industry and, seeking to obtain more profits, will enter the one that is expanding. A similar path will be followed by labor and other resources. This process will continue until the various markets produce the amount of each commodity that people want.

Competitive markets insure that prices, profits and wages will be neither too high nor too low. The increased supply of a product that is brought forth by businessmen seeking above-average profits will bring down prices and profits to their natural levels. Alternatively, when profits are below average, businessmen will exit from the industry and the subsequent reduction in supply will elevate both prices and profits.

A similar process occurs in labor markets. Suppose that there are two similar occupations but that one receives a higher wage than the other. This wage disparity will induce some to leave the lower-paying occupation and enter the one offering the higher reward. As the supply of labor in this occupation rises, its wage will decline while the decreased supply in the other occupation will have the opposite effect.

Note that all of this is taking place because people are expressing their self-interest through an impersonal, self-regulating market mechanism. Competition harnesses the drive of self-interest, it keeps prices close to costs, gives people choice, and guards against exploitation—a far cry from the regulation and planning of mercantilism. For those prejudiced against free markets and disposed toward regulation, Smith has some pungent remarks.

> The prejudices of some political writers against shopkeepers and tradesmen, are altogether without foundation. So far is it from being necessary, either to tax them, or to restrict their numbers, that they can never be multiplied so as to hurt the publick, though they may so as to hurt one another. The quantity of grocery goods, for example, which can be sold in a particular town, is limited by the demand of that town and its neighbourhood. The capital, therefore, which can be employed in the grocery trade cannot exceed what is sufficient to purchase that quantity. If this capital is divided between two different grocers, their competition will tend to make both of them sell cheaper, than if it were in the hands of one only; and if it were divided among twenty, their competition would be just so much the greater, and the chance of their combining together, in order to raise the price, just so much the less. Their competition might perhaps ruin some of themselves; but to take care of this is the business of the parties concerned, and it may safely be trusted to their discretion. It can never hurt either the consumer, or the producer; on the contrary, it must tend to

make the retailers both sell cheaper and
buy dearer, than if the whole trade was mo-
nopolized by one or two persons. Some of
them, perhaps, may sometimes decoy a
weak customer to buy what he has no occasion for. This evil, however, is of too little
importance to deserve the publick attention,
nor would it necessarily be prevented by re-
stricting their numbers. It is not the multitude of ale-houses, to give the most
suspicious example, that occasions a general
disposition to drunkenness among the common people; but that disposition arising
from other causes necessarily gives employment to a multitude of ale-houses.[8]

Smith believed that the benefits of competition
were ubiquitous and even extended to religion.

But if politics had never called in the aid
of religion, had the conquering party never
adopted the tenets of one sect more than
those of another, when it had gained the victory, it would probably have dealt equally
and impartially with all the different sects,
and have allowed every man to chuse his
own priest and his own religion as he
thought proper. There would in this case,
no doubt, have been a great multitude of
religious sects. Almost every different congregation might probably have made a little

sect by itself, or have entertained some peculiar tenets of its own. Each teacher would
no doubt have felt himself under the necessity of making the utmost exertion, and of
using every art both to preserve and to increase the number of his disciples. But as
every other teacher would have felt himself
under the same necessity, the success of no
one teacher, or sect of teachers, could have
been very great. The interested and active
zeal of religious teachers can be dangerous
and troublesome only where there is, either
but one sect tolerated in the society, or
where the whole of a large society is divided
into two or three great sects; the teachers
of each acting by concert, and under a regular discipline and subordination. But that
zeal must be altogether innocent where the
society is divided into two or three hundred,
or perhaps into as many thousand small
sects, of which no one could be considerable
enough to disturb the public tranquillity.
The teachers of each sect, seeing themselves
surrounded on all sides with more adversar-
ies than friends, would be obliged to learn
that candour and moderation which is so
seldom to be found among the teachers of
those great sects, whose tenets, being supported by the civil magistrate, are held in
veneration by almost all the inhabitants of
extensive kingdoms and empires, and who

therefore see nothing round them but fol-
lowers, disciples, and humble admirers. The
teachers of each little sect, finding themselves almost alone, would be obliged to respect those of almost every other sect, and
the concessions which they would mutually
find it both convenient and agreeable to
make to one another, might in time probably
reduce the doctrine of the greater part of
them to that pure and rational religion, free
from every mixture of absurdity, imposture,
or fanaticism, such as wise men have in all
ages of the world wished to see established;
but such as positive law has perhaps never
yet established, and probably never will establish in any country: because, with regard
to religion, positive law always has been, and
probably always will be, more or less influenced by popular superstition and enthusiasm. This plan of ecclesiastical government,
or more properly of no ecclesiastical government, was what the sect called Indepen-
dents, a sect no doubt of very wild
enthusiasts, proposed to establish in England towards the end of the civil war. If it
had been established, though of a very un-
philosophical origin, it would probably by
this time have been productive of the most
philosophical good temper and moderation
with regard to every sort of religious principle. It has been established in Pennsylvania,

where, though the Quakers happen to be the most numerous, the law in reality favours no one sect more than another, and it is there said to have been productive of this philosophical good temper and moderation.[9]

Smith, as a defender of free markets, is therefore an antagonist of monopoly.

A monopoly granted either to an individual or to a trading company has the same effect as a secret in trade or manufactures. The monopolists, by keeping the market constantly under-stocked, by never fully supplying the effectual demand, sell their commodities much above the natural price, and raise their emoluments, whether they consist in wages or profit, greatly above their natural rate.

The price of monopoly is upon every occasion the highest which can be got. The natural price, or the price of free competition, on the contrary, is the lowest which can be taken, not upon every occasion indeed, but for any considerable time altogether. The one is upon every occasion the highest which can be squeezed out of the buyers, or which, it is supposed, they will consent to give: The other is the lowest which the sellers can commonly afford to take, and at the same time continue their business.[10]

Monopoly, besides, is a great enemy to good management, which can never be universally established but in consequence of that free and universal competition which forces everybody to have recourse to it for the sake of self-defence.[11]

# PRODUCTIVITY AND THE DIVISION OF LABOR

In addition to giving us an understanding of how markets coordinate individual decision-making and allocate resources according to consumer desires, Smith also provided insight into other components of the growth process. One of these is productivity which refers to the quantity of a good that an individual and other factors of production can produce in a given period of time. Productivity was very important to Smith and he believed that its growth was primarily due to what he called the division of labor. Below are the first words of Chapter I in *The Wealth of Nations*.

> The greatest improvement in the productive powers of labour, and the greater part of the skill, dexterity, and judgment with which it is any where directed, or applied, seem to have been the effects of the division of labour.[12]

He then illustrated this with his famous description of a pin factory.

> To take an example, therefore, from a very trifling manufacture; but one in which the division of labour has been very often taken notice of, the trade of the pin maker; a workman not educated to this business (which the

division of labour has rendered a distinct trade), nor acquainted with the use of the machinery employed in it (to the invention of which the same division of labour has probably given occasion), could scarce, perhaps, with his utmost industry, make one pin in a day, and certainly could not make twenty. But in the way in which this business is now carried on, not only the whole work is a peculiar trade, but it is divided into a number of branches, of which the greater part are likewise peculiar trades. One man draws out the wire, another straights it, a third cuts it, a fourth points it, a fifth grinds it at the top for receiving the head; to make the head requires two or three distinct operations; to put it on, is a peculiar business, to whiten the pins is another; it is even a trade by itself to put them into the paper; and the important business of making a pin is, in this manner, divided into about eighteen distinct operations, which, in some manufactories, are all performed by distinct hands, though in others the same man will sometimes perform two or three of them. I have seen a small manufactory of this kind where ten men only were employed, and where some of them consequently performed two or three distinct operations. But though they were very poor, and therefore but indifferently accommodated with the necessary machinery, they could, when they exerted themselves, make among them about twelve pounds of pins in a day. There are in a pound upwards of four thousand pins of a middling size. Those ten persons, therefore, could make among them up- wards of forty-eight thousand pins in a day. Each person, therefore, making a tenth part of forty-eight thousand pins, might be considered as making four thousand eight hundred pins in a day. But if they had all wrought separately and independently, and without any of them having been educated to this peculiar business, they certainly could not each of them have made twenty, perhaps not one pin in a day; that is, certainly, not the two hundred and fortieth, perhaps not the four thousand eight hundredth part of what they are at present capable of performing, in consequence of a proper division and combination of their different operations.[13]

Smith offered three reasons for the productivity gains which stem from the division of labor.

This great increase of the quantity of work which, in consequence of the division of labour, the same number of people are capable of performing, is owing to three different circumstances; first to the increase of dexterity in every particular workman; secondly, to the saving of the time which is commonly lost in passing from one species of work to another; and lastly, to the invention of a great number of machines which facilitate and abridge labour, and enable one man to do the work of many.

First, the improvement of the dexterity of the workman necessarily increases the quantity of the work he can perform; and the division of labour, by reducing every man's business to some one simple operation, and by making this operation the sole employment of his life, necessarily increases very much the dexterity of the workman. A common smith, who, though accustomed to handle the hammer, has never been used to make nails, if upon some particular occasion he is obliged to attempt it, will scarce, I am assured, be able to make above two or three hundred nails in a day, and those too very bad ones. A smith who has been accustomed to make nails, but whose sole or principal business has not been that of a nailer, can seldom with his utmost diligence make more than eight hundred or a thousand nails in a day. I have seen several boys under twenty years of age who had never exercised any other trade but that of making nails, and who, when they exerted themselves, could make, each of them, upwards of two thousand three hundred nails in a day. The making of a nail, however, is by no means one of the simplest operations. The same person blows the bellows, stirs or mends the fire as there is occasion, heats the iron, and forges every part of the nail: In forging the head too he is obliged to change his tools. The different operations into which the making of a pin, or of a metal button, is subdivided, are all of them much more simple, and the dexterity of the person, of whose life it has been the sole business to perform them, is usually much greater. The rapidity with which some of the operations of those manufactures are performed, exceeds what the human hand could, by those who had never seen them, be supposed capable of acquiring.

Secondly, the advantage which is gained by saving the time commonly lost in passing from one sort of work to another, is much greater than we should at first view be apt to imagine it. It is impossible to pass very quickly from one kind of work to another; that is carried on in a different place, and with quite different tools. A country weaver, who cultivates a small farm, must lose a good deal of time in passing from his loom to the field, and from the field to his loom. When the two trades can be carried on in the same workhouse, the loss of time is no doubt much less. It is even in this case,

however, very considerable. A man commonly saunters a little in turning his hand
from one sort of employment to another.
When he first begins the new work he is
seldom very keen and hearty; his mind, as
they say, does not go to it, and for some time
he rather trifles than applies to good purpose. The habit of sauntering and of indo-
lent careless application, which is naturally,
or rather necessarily acquired by every
country workman who is obliged to change
his work and his tools every half hour, and
to apply his hand to twenty different ways
almost every day of his life; renders him almost always slothful and lazy, and incapable of any vigorous application even on the
most pressing occasions. Independent,
therefore, of his deficiency in point of dexterity, this cause alone must always reduce
considerably the quantity of work which he
is capable of performing.

Thirdly, and lastly, every body must be sensible how much labour is facilitated and
abridged by the application of proper machinery. It is unnecessary to give any example. I shall only observe, therefore, that the
invention of all those machines by which labour is so much facilitated and abridged,
seems to have been originally owing to the
division of labour. Men are much more likely
to discover easier and readier methods of

attaining any object, when the whole attention of their minds is directed towards that
single object, than when it is dissipated
among a great variety of things. But in consequence of the division of labour, the whole
of every man's attention comes naturally to
be directed towards some one very simple
object. It is naturally to be expected, therefore, that some one or other of those who
are employed in each particular branch of
labour should soon find out easier and
readier methods of performing their own
particular work, wherever the nature of it
admits of such improvement. A great part
of the machines made use of in those manufactures in which labour is most subdivided, were originally the inventions of
common workmen, who, being each of them
employed in some very simple operation,
naturally turned their thoughts towards
finding out easier and readier methods of
performing it. Whoever has been much accustomed to visit such manufactures, must
frequently have been shewn very pretty machines, which were the inventions of such
workmen, in order to facilitate and quicken
their own particular part of the work.[14]

Trade, while not as vital to Smith as it was to the
mercantilists, nonetheless was important to him because it widened the market and thereby allowed

increased productivity. In fact, Chapter III of Book I is titled "That The Division Of Labour Is Limited By The Extent Of The Market."[15] In other words, if the demand for a product is small, the worker might best produce it all by himself because a single machine would be unable to perform so many complex operations. However, when the demand for the product is great, then the task of producing it can be broken down and simplified, machinery can be introduced and productivity increased. Smith was aware that the discovery of America had the effect of widening the market.

> By opening a new and inexhaustible market to all the commodities of Europe, it gave occasion to new divisions of labour and improvements of art, which, in the narrow circle of the ancient commerce, could never have taken place for want of a market to take off the greater part of their produce. The productive powers of labour were improved, and its produce increased in all the different countries of Europe, and together with it the real revenue and wealth of the inhabitants. The commodities of Europe were almost all new to America, and many of those of America were new to Europe. A new set of exchanges, therefore, began to take place which had never been thought of before, and which should naturally have

proved as advantageous to the new, as it certainly did to the old continent.[16]

Smith wrote at the very beginning of the industrial revolution before the factory system became important. He did not foresee the tremendous advances in technology and real capital formation that would take place and so he believed that productivity gains would be mainly the result of the division of labor which comes about naturally through self-interest and ". . . the propensity to truck, barter, and exchange one thing with another."[17]

## CAPITAL ACCUMULATION

Capital accumulation was important to Smith. The word had several meanings to him, including financial savings; food, clothing and other provisions that were necessary to maintain labor; and tools and machinery. Frugality was the source of capital, and the growth of the latter contributed to economic development by allowing higher employment and by providing more tools and equipment with which to work.

Capitals are increased by parsimony, and diminished by prodigality and misconduct.

Whatever a person saves from his revenue he adds to his capital, and either employs it himself in maintaining an additional number of productive hands, or enables some other person to do so, by lending it to him for an interest, that is, for a share of the profits. As the capital of an individual can be increased only by what he saves from his annual revenue or his annual gains, so the capital of a society, which is the same with that of all the individuals who compose it, can be increased only in the same manner.

Parsimony, and not industry, is the immediate cause of the increase of capital. Industry, indeed, provides the subject which parsimony accumulates. But whatever industry might acquire, if parsimony did not save and store up, the capital would never be the greater.

Parsimony, by increasing the fund which is destined for the maintenance of productive hands, tends to increase the number of those hands whose labour adds to the value of the subject upon which it is bestowed. It tends therefore to increase the exchangeable value of the annual produce of the land and labour of the country. It puts into motion an additional quantity of industry, which gives an additional value to the annual produce.[18]

By what a frugal man annually saves, he not only affords maintenance to an additional number of productive hands, for that or the ensuing year, but like the founder of a public workhouse, he establishes as it were a perpetual fund for the maintenance of an equal number in all times to come. The perpetual allotment and destination of this fund, indeed, is not always guarded by any positive law, by any trust-right or deed of mortmain. It is always guarded, however, by a very powerful principle, the plain and evident interest of every individual to whom any share of it shall ever belong. No part of it can ever afterwards be employed to maintain any but productive hands, without an evident loss to the person who thus perverts it from its proper destination.

The prodigal perverts it in this manner. By not confining his expence within his income, he encroaches upon his capital. Like him who perverts the revenues of some pious foundation to profane purposes, he pays the wages of idleness with those funds which the frugality of his forefathers had, as it were, consecrated to the maintenance of industry. By diminishing the funds destined for the employment of productive labour, he necessarily diminishes, so far as it depends upon him, the quantity of that labour which adds a value to the subject upon which it is bestowed, and, consequently, the value of the annual produce of the land and labour of the whole country, the real wealth and revenue of its inhabitants. If the prodigality of some was not compensated by the frugality of others, the conduct of every prodigal, by feeding the idle with the bread of the industrious, tends not only to beggar himself, but to impoverish his country.[19]

# ECONOMIC GROWTH AND ITS BENEFICIARIES

Smith did not believe that the economic progress which he envisioned would follow a smooth and steady path. He believed that the accumulation of capital would expand the demand for labor, causing wages to be higher. This, in turn, would increase the cost of production and reduce profits, which were an important source of capital accumulation. However, the dilemma was not without a solution. In those days, the mortality rate for children was very high, and Smith thought that higher wages would permit more children to reach maturity. A larger population would bring forth a more sizeable labor force. Competition among this group for employment would depress wages and thereby cause profits to ascend and capital to grow. Although he was not referring to the business cycle as we understand it today, Smith did believe there would be fluctuations in economic activity. In the long run, however, the overall trend would be in an upward direction.

People in the eighteenth century lacked the conveniences we take for granted today. Instead there was widespread poverty, illiteracy and early death. Nevertheless, Smith perceived his era to represent a great improvement over earlier periods. The fruits of growth were evident and they would be even greater if his system of natural liberty was put in place.

Observe the accommodation of the most common artificer or day-labourer in a civilized and thriving country, and you will perceive that the number of people of whose industry a part, though but a small part, has been employed in procuring him this accommodation, exceeds all computation. The woollen coat, for example, which covers the day-labourer, as coarse and rough as it may appear, is the produce of the joint labour of a great multitude of workmen. The shepherd, the sorter of the wool, the wool-comber or carder, the dyer, the scribbler, the spinner, the weaver, the fuller, the dresser, with many others, must all join their different arts in order to complete even this homely production. How many merchants and carriers, besides, must have been employed in transporting the materials from some of those workmen to others who often live in a very distant part of the country! how much commerce and navigation in particular, how many ship-builders, sailors, sail-makers, rope-makers, must have been employed in order to bring together the different drugs made use of by the dyer, which often come from the remotest corners of the world! What a variety of labour too is necessary in order to produce the tools of the meanest of those workmen! To say nothing of such complicated machines as the ship of the sailor, the mill of the fuller, or even the loom of the weaver, let us consider only what a variety of labour is requisite in order to form that very simple machine, the shears with which the shepherd clips the wool. The miner, the builder of the furnace for smelting the ore, the feller of the timber, the burner of the charcoal to be made use of in the smelting-house, the brick-maker, the brick-layer, the workmen who attend the furnace, the mill-wright, the forger, the smith, must all of them join their different arts in order to produce them. Were we to examine, in the same manner, all the different parts of his dress and household furniture, the coarse linen shirt which he wears next to his skin, the shoes which cover his feet, the bed which he lies on, and all the different parts which compose it, the kitchen-grate at which he prepares his victuals, the coals which he makes use of for that purpose, dug from the bowels of the earth, and brought to him perhaps by a long sea and a long land carriage, all the other utensils of his kitchen, all the furniture of his table, the knives and forks, the earthen or pewter plates upon which he serves up and divides his victuals, the different hands employed in preparing his bread and his beer, the glass window which lets in the heat and the light, and keeps out the wind and the rain, with all the knowledge and art requisite for preparing that beautiful and happy invention, without which these northern parts of the world could scarce have afforded a very comfortable habitation, together with the tools of all the different workmen employed in producing those different conveniences; if we examine, I say, all these things, and consider what a variety of labour is employed about each of them, we shall be sensible that without the assistance and cooperation of many thousands, the very meanest person in a civilized country could not be provided, even according to what we very falsely imagine, the easy and simple manner in which he is commonly accommodated. Compared, indeed, with the more extravagant luxury of the great, his accommodation must no doubt appear extremely simple and easy; and yet it may be true, perhaps, that the accommodation of an European prince does not always so much exceed that of an industrious and frugal peasant, as the accommodation of the latter exceeds that of many an African king, the absolute master of the lives and liberties of ten thousand naked savages.[20]

Smith believed that the benefits of the division of labor and economic growth were widely shared.

It is the great multiplication of the pro-
ductions of all the different arts, in consequence of the division of labour, which
occasions, in a well-governed society, that
universal opulence which extends itself to
the lowest ranks of the people. Every workman has a great quantity of his own work
to dispose of beyond what he himself has
occasion for; and every other workman
being exactly in the same situation, he is
enabled to exchange a great quantity of his
own goods for a great quantity, or, what
comes to the same thing, for the price of a
great quantity of theirs. He supplies them
abundantly with what they have occasion
for, and they accommodate him as amply
with what he has occasion for, and a general
plenty diffuses itself through all the different ranks of the society.[21]

He even developed a trickle-down theory of how
expenditures by the rich on durable goods had national benefits.

As the one mode of expence is more favourable than the other to the opulence of an individual, so is it likewise to that of a nation.
The houses, the furniture, the clothing of
the rich, in a little time, become useful to
the inferior and middling ranks of people.
They are able to purchase them when their

superiors grow weary of them, and the general accommodation of the whole people is thus gradually improved, when this mode of expence becomes universal among men of fortune. In countries which have long been rich, you will frequently find the inferior ranks of people in possession both of houses and furniture perfectly good and entire, but of which neither the one could have been built, nor the other have been made for their use. What was formerly a seat of the family of Seymour, is now an inn upon the Bath road. The marriage-bed of James the First of Great Britain, which his Queen brought with her from Denmark, as a present fit for a sovereign to make to a sovereign, was, a few years ago, the ornament of an ale-house at Dunfermline. In some ancient cities, which either have been long stationary, or have gone somewhat to decay, you will sometimes scarce find a single house which could have been built for its present inhabitants. If you go into those houses too, you will frequently find many excellent, though antiquated pieces of furniture, which are still very fit for use, and which could as little have been made for them. Noble palaces, magnificent villas, great collections of books, statues, pictures, and other curiosities, are frequently both an ornament and an honour, not only to the neighbourhood, but to the whole country to which they belong. Versailles is an ornament and an honour to France, Stowe and Wilton to England. Italy still continues to command some sort of veneration by the number of monuments of this kind which it possesses, though the wealth which produced them has decayed, and though the genius which planned them seems to be extinguished, perhaps from not having the same employment.[22]

Smith thought that workers more than any other group would benefit the most from an expanding economy because the demand for labor would rise.

It is not the actual greatness of national wealth, but its continual increase, which occasions a rise in the wages of labour. It is not, accordingly, in the richest countries, but in the most thriving, or in those which are growing rich the fastest, that the wages of labour are highest. England is certainly, in the present time, a much richer country than any part of North America. The wages of labour, however, are much higher in North America than in any part of England.[23]

The following words might well be heeded by today's "no growth" apostles.

It deserves to be remarked, perhaps, that
it is in the progressive state, while the society is advancing to the further acquisition,
rather than when it has acquired its full
complement of riches, that the condition of
the labouring poor, of the great body of the
people, seems to be the happiest and the
most comfortable. It is hard in the stationary, and miserable in the declining state.
The progressive state is in reality the cheer-
ful and the hearty state to all the different
orders of the society. The stationary is dull;
the declining melancholy.[24]

In contrast to the mercantilists, Smith held the
radical ideas that all should share in progress and
that high wages were desirable.

Is this improvement in the circumstances
of the lower ranks of the people to be regarded as an advantage or as an inconveniency to the society? The answer seems at
first sight abundantly plain. Servants,
labourers and workmen of different kinds,
make up the far greater part of every great
political society. But what improves the circumstances of the greater part can never be
regarded as an inconveniency to the whole.
No society can surely be flourishing and
happy, of which the far greater part of the
members are poor and miserable. It is but

equity, besides, that they who feed, cloath and lodge the whole body of the people, should have such a share of the produce of their own labour as to be themselves tolerably well fed, cloathed and lodged.[25]

# CHAPTER 5

## The International Economy

Adam Smith believed that the benefits of exchange extended to the international arena, and consistent with his attitude toward monopoly, he staunchly supported free trade. Contrary to the antagonistic philosophy of mercantilism, he posited a harmony of interest.

### INTERNATIONAL TRADE

By restraining, either by high duties, or by absolute prohibitions, the importation of such goods from foreign countries as can be produced at home, the monopoly of the home market is more or less secured to the domestic industry employed in producing them. Thus the prohibition of importing either live cattle or salt provisions from foreign countries secures to the graziers of Great Britain the monopoly of the home market for butcher's meat. The high duties upon the importation of corn, which in times of moderate plenty amount to a prohibition, give a like advantage to the growers of that commodity. The prohibition of the importation of foreign woollens is equally favourable to the woollen manufacturers. The silk manufacture, though altogether employed upon foreign materials, has lately obtained the same advantage. The linen manufacture has not yet obtained it, but is making great strides towards it. Many other sorts of manufacturers have, in the same manner, obtained in Great Britain, either altogether, or very nearly a monopoly against their countrymen. The variety of goods of which the importation into Great Britain is prohibited, either absolutely, or under certain circumstances, greatly exceeds what can easily be suspected by those who are not well acquainted with the laws of the customs.

That this monopoly of the home-market frequently gives great encouragement to that particular species of industry which enjoys it, and frequently turns towards that employment a greater share of both the labour and stock of the society than would otherwise have gone to it, cannot be doubted. But whether it tends either to increase the general industry of the society, or to give it the most advantageous direction, is not, perhaps, altogether so evident.

The general industry of the society never can exceed what the capital of the society can employ. As the number of workmen that can be kept in employment by any particular person must bear a certain proportion to his capital, so the number of those that can be continually employed by all the members of

a great society, must bear a certain proportion to the whole capital of that society, and
never can exceed that proportion. No regulation of commerce can increase the quantity of industry in any society beyond what
its capital can maintain. It can only divert
a part of it into a direction into which it
might not otherwise have gone; and it is by
no means certain that this artificial direction is likely to be more advantageous to
the society than that into which it would
have gone of its own accord.[1]

To give the monopoly of the home-market
to the produce of domestic industry, in any
particular art or manufacture, is in some
measure to direct private people in what
manner they ought to employ their capitals,
and must, in almost all cases, be either a
useless or a hurtful regulation. If the produce of domestic can be brought there as
cheap as that of foreign industry, the regulation is evidently useless. If it cannot, it
must generally be hurtful. It is the maxim
of every prudent master of a family, never
to attempt to make at home what it will
cost him more to make than to buy. The taylor does not attempt to make his own shoes,
but buys them of the shoemaker. The shoemaker does not attempt to make his own
clothes, but employs a taylor. The farmer

attempts to make neither the one nor the other, but employs those different artificers. All of them find it for their interest to employ their whole industry in a way in which they have some advantage over their neighbours, and to purchase with a part of its produce, or what is the same thing, with the price of a part of it, whatever else they have occasion for.

What is prudence in the conduct of every private family, can scarce be folly in that of a great kingdom. If a foreign country can supply us with a commodity cheaper than we ourselves can make it, better buy it of them with some part of the produce of our own industry, employed in a way in which we have some advantage. The general industry of the country, being always in proportion to the capital which employs it, will not thereby be diminished, no more than that of the above-mentioned artificers; but only left to find out the way in which it can be employed with the greatest advantage. It is certainly not employed to the greatest advantage, when it is thus directed towards an object which it can buy cheaper than it can make. The value of its annual produce is certainly more or less diminished, when it is thus turned away from producing commodities evidently of more value than the commodity which it is directed to produce.[2]

The natural advantages which one country has over another in producing particular commodities are sometimes so great, that it is acknowledged by all the world to be in vain to struggle with them. By means of glasses, hotbeds, and hotwalls, very good grapes can be raised in Scotland, and very good wine too can be made of them at about thirty times the expence for which at least equally good can be brought from foreign countries. Would it be a reasonable law to prohibit the importation of all foreign wines, merely to encourage the making of claret and burgundy in Scotland? But if there would be a manifest absurdity in turning towards any employment, thirty times more of the capital and industry of the country, than would be necessary to purchase from foreign countries an equal quantity of the commodities wanted, there must be an absurdity, though not altogether so glaring, yet exactly of the same kind, in turning towards any such employment a thirtieth, or even a three hundredth part more of either. Whether the advantages which one country has over another, be natural or acquired, is in this respect of no consequence. As long as the one country has those advantages, and the other wants them, it will always be more advantageous for the latter, rather to buy of the former than to make. It is an acquired advantage only, which one artificer has over his neighbour, who exercises another trade; and yet they both find it more advantageous to buy of one another, than to make what does not belong to their particular trades.[3]

Adam Smith, however, was not an unqualified defender of free trade. He allowed for two exceptions.

There seem, however, to be two cases in which it will generally be advantageous to lay some burden upon foreign, for the encouragement of domestic industry.

The first is, when some particular sort of industry is necessary for the defence of the country. The defence of Great Britain, for example, depends very much upon the number of its sailors and shipping. The act of navigation, therefore, very properly endeavours to give the sailors and shipping of Great Britain the monopoly of the trade of their own country, in some cases, by absolute prohibitions, and in others by heavy burdens upon the shipping of foreign countries.[4]

The act of navigation is not favourable to foreign commerce, or to the growth of that opulence which can arise from it. The interest of a nation in its commercial relations to foreign nations is, like that of a merchant with regard to the different people with whom he deals, to buy as cheap and to sell as dear as possible. But it will be most likely to buy cheap, when by the most perfect freedom of trade it encourages all nations to bring to it the goods which it has occasion to purchase; and, for the same reason, it will be most likely to sell dear, when its markets are thus filled with the greatest number of buyers. The act of navigation, it is true, lays no burden upon foreign ships that come to export the produce of British industry. Even the ancient aliens duty, which used to be paid upon all goods exported as well as imported, has, by several subsequent acts, been taken of from the greater part of the articles of exportation. But if foreigners, either by prohibitions or high duties, are hindered from coming to sell, they cannot always afford to come to buy; because coming without a cargo, they must lose the freight from their own country to Great Britain. By diminishing the number of sellers, therefore, we necessarily diminish that of buyers, and are thus likely not only to buy foreign goods dearer, but to sell our own cheaper, than if there was a more perfect freedom of trade. As defence, however, is of much more importance than opulence, the act of navigation is, perhaps, the wisest of all the commercial regulations of England.

The second case, in which it will generally be advantageous to lay some burden upon foreign for the encouragement of domestic industry, is, when some tax is imposed at home upon the produce of the latter. In this case, it seems reasonable that an equal tax should be imposed upon the like produce of the former. This would not give the monopoly of the home market to domestic industry, nor turn towards a particular employment a greater share of the stock and labour of the country, than what would naturally go to it. It would only hinder any part of what would naturally go to it from being turned away by the tax, into a less natural direction, and would leave the competition between foreign and domestic industry, after the tax, as nearly as possible upon the same footing as before it. In Great Britain, when any such tax is laid upon the produce of domestic industry, it is usual at the same time, in order to stop the clamorous complaints of our merchants and manufacturers, that they will be undersold at home, to lay a much heavier duty upon the importation of all foreign goods of the same kind.[5]

Smith also considered the strategy of retaliation when a foreign country restricted the importation of a nation's produce. He believed retaliation to be warranted if it induced the offending nation to lower its barriers, but if that did not happen such a policy caused more harm than good.

The case in which it may sometimes be a matter of deliberation how far it is proper to continue the free importation of certain foreign goods, is, when some foreign nation restrains by high duties or prohibitions the importation of some of our manufactures into their country. Revenge in this case naturally dictates retaliation, and that we should impose the like duties and prohibitions upon the importation of some or all of their manufactures into ours. Nations accordingly seldom fail to retaliate in this manner.[6]

There may be good policy in retaliations of this kind, when there is a probability that they will procure the repeal of the high duties or prohibitions complained of . The recovery of a great foreign market will generally more than compensate the transitory inconveniency of paying dearer during a short time for some sorts of goods. To judge whether such retaliations are likely to produce such an effect, does not, perhaps, belong so much to the science of a legislator, whose deliberations ought to be governed by general principles which are always the same, as to the skill of that insidious and crafty animal, vulgarly called a statesman or politician, whose councils are directed by the momentary fluctuations of affairs. When there is no probability that any such repeal can be procured, it seems a bad method of compensating the injury done to certain classes of our people, to do another injury ourselves, not only to those classes, but to almost all other classes of them. When our neighbours prohibit some manufacture of ours, we generally prohibit, not only the same, for that alone would seldom affect them considerably, but some other manufacture of theirs. This may no doubt give encouragement to some particular class of workmen among ourselves, and by excluding some of their rivals, may enable them to raise their price in the home-market. Those workmen, however, who suffered by our neighbours prohibition will not be benefited by ours. On the contrary, they and almost all the other classes of our citizens will thereby be obliged to pay dearer than before for certain goods. Every such law, therefore, imposes a real tax upon the whole country, not in favour of that particular class of workmen who were injured by our neighbours prohibition, but of some other class.[7]

Smith then assessed the desirability of removing protective policies which already were in place and suggested that this be done gently.

The case in which it may sometimes be a matter of deliberation, how far, or in what manner, it is proper to restore the free importation of foreign goods, after it has been for some time interrupted, is, when particular manufactures, by means of high duties or prohibitions upon all foreign goods which can come into competition with them, have been so far extended as to employ a great multitude of hands. Humanity may in this case require that the freedom of trade should be restored only by slow gradations, and with a good deal of reserve and circumspection. Were those high duties and prohibitions taken away all at once, cheaper foreign goods of the same kind might be poured so fast into the home market, as to deprive all at once many thousands of our people of their ordinary employment and means of subsistence. The disorder which this would occasion might no doubt be very considerable. It would in all probability, however, be much less than is commonly imagined, for the two following reasons:

First, all those manufactures, of which any part is commonly exported to other European countries without a bounty, could be very little affected by the freest importation of foreign goods. Such manufactures must be sold as cheap abroad as any other foreign goods of the same quality and kind, and consequently must be sold cheaper at home. They would still, therefore, keep possession of the home market, and though a capricious man of fashion might sometimes prefer foreign wares, merely because they were foreign, to cheaper and better goods of the same kind that were made at home, this folly could, from the nature of things, extend to so few, that it could make no sensible impression upon the general employment of the people.[8]

He maintained that removing the restrictions on free trade would make it easier for people to find jobs.

Secondly, though a great number of people should, by thus restoring the freedom of trade, be thrown all at once out of their ordinary employment and common method of subsistence, it would by no means follow that they would thereby be deprived either of employment or subsistence. By the reduction of the army and navy at the end of the late war, more than a hundred thousand soldiers and seamen, a number equal to what is employed in the greatest manufactures, were all at once thrown out of their ordinary employment; but though they no doubt suffered some inconveniency, they were not thereby deprived of all employment and subsistence. The greater part of the seamen, it is probable, gradually betook themselves to the merchant-service as they could find occasion, and in the meantime both they and the soldiers were absorbed in the great mass of the people, and employed in a great variety of occupations. Not only no great convulsion, but no sensible disorder arose from so great a change in the situation of more than a hundred thousand men, all accustomed to the use of arms, and many of them to rapine and plunder. The number of vagrants was scarce any-where sensibly increased by it, even the wages of labour were not reduced by it in any occupation, so far as I have been able to learn, except in that of seamen in the merchant-service. But if we compare together the habits of a soldier and of any sort of manufacturer, we shall find that those of the latter do not tend so much to disqualify him from being employed in a new trade, as those of the former from being employed in any. The manufacturer has always been accustomed to look for his subsistence from his labour only: the soldier to expect it from his pay. Application and industry have been familiar to the one; idleness and dissipation to the other. But it is surely much easier to change the direction of industry from one sort of labour to another, than to turn idleness and dissipation to any. To the greater part of manufactures besides, it has already been observed, there are other collateral manufactures of so similar a nature, that a workman can easily transfer his industry from one of them to another. The greater part of such workmen too are occasionally employed in country labour. The stock which employed them in a particular manufacture before, will still remain in the country to employ an equal number of people in some other way. The capital of the country remaining the same, the demand for labour will likewise be the same, or very nearly the same, though it may be exerted in different places and for different occupations. Soldiers and seamen, indeed, when discharged from the king's service, are at liberty to exercise any trade, within any town or place of Great Britain or Ireland. Let the same natural liberty of exercising what species of industry they please, be restored to all his majesty's subjects, in the same manner as to soldiers and seamen; that is, break down the exclusive privileges of corporations, and repeal the statute of apprenticeship, both which are real encroachments upon natural liberty, and add to

these the repeal of the law of settlements,
so that a poor workman, when thrown out
of employment either in one trade or in one
place, may seek for it in another trade or
in another place, without the fear either of
a prosecution or of a removal, and neither
the public nor the individuals will suffer
much more from the occasional disbanding
some particular classes of manufacturers,
than from that of soldiers. Our manufacturers have no doubt great merit with their
country, but they cannot have more than
those who defend it with their blood, nor
deserve to be treated with more delicacy.[9]

Smith was no ivory-towered utopian who believed
that the force of logic would bring about completely
free trade. He was much aware of vested interest
and the pressures brought to bear on those who
sought to alter existing policy.

To expect, indeed, that the freedom of trade
should ever be entirely restored in Great
Britain, is as absurd as to expect that an
Oceana or Utopia should ever be established
in it. Not only the prejudices of the public,
but what is much more unconquerable, the
private interests of many individuals, irre-
sistibly oppose it. Were the officers of the
army to oppose with the same zeal and una-
nimity any reduction in the number of forces,

with which master manufacturers set themselves against every law that is likely to increase the number of their rivals in the home market; were the former to animate their soldiers, in the same manner as the latter enflame their workmen, to attack with violence and outrage the proposers of any such regulations; to attempt to reduce the army would be as dangerous as it has now become to attempt to diminish in any respect the monopoly which our manufacturers have obtained against us. This monopoly has so much increased the number of some particular tribes of them, that, like an overgrown standing army, they have become formidable to the government, and upon many occasions intimidate the legislature. The member of parliament who supports every proposal for strengthening this monopoly, is sure to acquire not only the reputation of understanding trade, but great popularity and influence with an order of men whose numbers and wealth render them of great importance. If he opposes them, on the contrary, and still more if he has authority enough to be able to thwart them, neither the most acknowledged probity, nor the highest rank, nor the greatest public services, can protect him from the most infamous abuse and detraction, from personal insults, nor sometimes from real danger, arising from the insolent outrage of furious and disappointed monopolists.

The undertaker of a great manufacture, who, by the home markets being suddenly laid open to the competition of foreigners, should be obliged to abandon his trade, would no doubt suffer very considerably. That part of his capital which had usually been employed in purchasing materials and in paying his workmen, might, without much difficulty, perhaps, find another employment. But that part of it which was fixed in workhouses, and in the instruments of trade, could scarce be disposed of without considerable loss. The equitable regard, therefore, to his interest requires that changes of this kind should never be introduced suddenly, but slowly, gradually, and after a very long warning. The legislature, were it possible that its deliberations could be always directed, not by the clamorous importunity of partial interests, but by an extensive view of the general good, ought upon this very account, perhaps, to be particularly careful neither to establish any new monopolies of this kind, nor to extend further those which are already established. Every such regulation introduces some degree of real disorder into the constitution of the state, which it will be difficult afterwards to cure without occasioning another disorder.[10]

Smith gave considerable attention to specific policies that interfered with trade. Using alcoholic beverages as an illustration, he attacked the argument that a nation should award preferential treatment to a country because it was a good customer.

It is a losing trade, it is said, which a workman carries on with the alehouse; and the trade which a manufacturing nation would naturally carry on with a wine country, may be considered as a trade of the same nature. I answer, that the trade with the alehouse is not necessarily a losing trade. In its own nature it is just as advantageous as any other, though, perhaps, somewhat more liable to be abused. The employment of a brewer, and even that of a retailer of fermented liquors, are as necessary divisions of labour as any other. It will generally be more advantageous for a workman to buy of the brewer the quantity he has occasion for, than to brew it himself, and if he is a poor workman, it will generally be more advantageous for him to buy it, by little and little, of the retailer, than a large quantity of the brewer. He may no doubt buy too much of either, as he may of any other dealers in his neighbourhood, of the butcher, if he is a glutton, or of the draper, if he affects to be a beau among his companions. It is advantageous to the great body of workmen, notwithstanding, that all these trades should be free, though this freedom may be abused in all of them, and is more likely to be so, perhaps, in some than in others. Though individuals, besides, may sometimes ruin their fortunes by an excessive consumption of fermented liquors, there seems to be no risk that a nation should do so. Though in every country there are many people who spend upon such liquors more than they can afford, there are always many more who spend less. It deserved to be remarked too, that, if we consult experience, the cheapness of wine seems to be a cause, not of drunkenness, but of sobriety. The inhabitants of the wine countries are in general the soberest people in Europe; witness the Spaniards, the Italians, and the inhabitants of the southern provinces of France. People are seldom guilty of excess in what is their daily fare. Nobody affects the character of liberality and good fellowship, by being profuse of a liquor which is as cheap as small beer. On the contrary, in the countries which, either from excessive heat or cold, produce no grapes, and where wine consequently is dear and a rarity, drunkenness is a common vice, as among the northern nations, and all those who live between the tropics, the negroes, for example, on the coast of Guinea.

When a French regiment comes from some of the northern provinces of France, where wine is somewhat dear, to be quartered in the southern, where it is very cheap, the soldiers, I have frequently heard it observed, are at first debauched by the cheapness and novelty of good wine; but after a few months residence, the greater part of them become as sober as the rest of the inhabitants. Were the duties upon foreign wines, and the excises upon malt, beer, and ale, to be taken away all at once, it might, in the same manner, occasion in Great Britain a pretty general and temporary drunkenness among the middling and inferior ranks of people, which would probably be soon followed by a permanent and almost universal sobriety. At present drunkenness is by no means the vice of people of fashion, or of those who can easily afford the most expensive liquors. A gentleman drunk with ale, has scarce ever been seen among us. The restraints upon the wine trade in Great Britain, besides, do not so much seem calculated to hinder the people from going, if I may say so, to the alehouse, as from going where they can buy the best and cheapest liquor. They favour the wine trade of Portugal, and discourage that of France. The Portuguese, it is said, indeed, are better customers for our manufactures than the

French, and should therefore be encouraged in preference to them. As they give us their custom, it is pretended, we should give them ours. The sneaking arts of underling trades-men are thus erected into political maxims for the conduct of a great empire; for it is the most underling tradesmen only who make it a rule to employ chiefly their own customers. A great trader purchases his goods always where they are cheapest and best, without regard to any little interest of this kind.[11]

He was particularly wary of the mercantile policy of giving bounties (subsidies) to export industries.

Bounties upon exportation are, in Great Britain, frequently petitioned for, and some-times granted to the produce of particular branches of domestic industry. By means of them our merchants and manufacturers, it is pretended, will be enabled to sell their goods as cheap or cheaper than their rivals in the foreign market. A greater quantity, it is said, will thus be exported, and the bal-ance of trade consequently turned more in favour of our own country. We cannot give our workmen a monopoly in the foreign, as we have done in the home market. We can-not force foreigners to buy their goods, as we have done our own countrymen. The next best expedient, it has been thought, therefore, is to pay them for buying. It is in this manner that the mercantile system proposes to enrich the whole country, and to put money into all our pockets by means of the balance of trade.

Bounties, it is allowed, ought to be given to those branches of trade only which cannot be carried on without them. But every branch of trade in which the merchant can sell his goods for a price which replaces to him, with the ordinary profits of stock, the whole capital employed in preparing and sending them to market, can be carried on without a bounty. Every such branch is evidently upon a level with all the other branches of trade which are carried on without bounties, and cannot therefore require one more than they. Those trades only require bounties in which the merchant is obliged to sell his goods for a price which does not replace to him his capital, together with the ordinary profit; or in which he is obliged to sell them for less than it really costs him to send them to market. The bounty is given in order to make up this loss, and to encourage him to continue, or perhaps to begin, a trade of which the expence is supposed to be greater than the returns, of which every operation eats up a part of the capital employed in it, and which is of such a nature, that, if all other trades resembled it, there would soon be no capital left in the country.

The trades, it is to be observed, which are carried on by means of bounties, are the only ones which can be carried on between two nations for any considerable time together, in such a manner as that one of them shall always and regularly lose, or sell its goods for less than it really costs to send them to market. But if the bounty did not repay to the merchant what he would otherwise lose upon the price of his goods, his own interest would soon oblige him to employ his stock in another way, or to find out a trade in which the price of the goods would replace to him, with the ordinary profit, the capital employed in sending them to market. The effect of bounties, like that of all the other expedients of the mercantile system, can only be to force the trade of a country into a channel much less advantageous than that in which it would naturally run of its own accord.[12]

Below is Smith's reply to those who contended that subsidies really are beneficial to a nation.

I answer, that whatever extension of the foreign market can be occasioned by the bounty, must, in every particular year, be altogether at the expence of the home market; as every bushel of corn which is exported by means of the bounty, and which would not have been exported without the bounty, would have remained in the home market to increase the consumption, and to lower the price of that commodity. The corn bounty, it is to be observed, as well as every other bounty upon exportation, imposes two different taxes upon the people; first, the tax which they are obliged to contribute, in order to pay the bounty; and secondly, the tax which arises from the advanced price of the commodity in the home market, and which, as the whole body of the people are purchasers of corn, must in this particular commodity, be paid by the whole body of the people. In this particular commodity, therefore, this second tax is by much the heaviest of the two.[13]

Here, also, Smith qualified his position and would allow subsidies to be awarded for purposes of national defense. However, he noted that this was subject to abuse and should be done with caution.

If any particular manufacture was necessary, indeed, for the defence of the society, it might not always be prudent to depend upon our neighbours for the supply; and if such manufacture could not otherwise be supported at home, it might not be unreasonable that all the other branches of industry should be taxed in order to support it. The bounties upon the exportation of British-made sail-cloth, and British-made gun-powder, may, perhaps, both be vindicated upon this principle.

But though it can very seldom be reasonable to tax the industry of the great body of the people, in order to support that of some particular class of manufacturers; yet in the wantonness of great prosperity, when the public enjoys a greater revenue than it knows well what to do with, to give such bounties to favourite manufactures, may, perhaps, be as natural, as to incur any other idle expence. In public, as well as in private expences, great wealth may, perhaps, frequently be admitted as an apology for great folly. But there must surely be something more than ordinary absurdity, in continuing such profusion in times of general difficulty and distress.[14]

Treaties granting monopoly privileges also were taken to task.

When a nation binds itself by treaty either to permit the entry of certain goods from one foreign country which it prohibits from all others, or to exempt the goods of one country from duties to which it subjects those of all others, the country, or at least the merchants and manufacturers of the country, whose commerce is so favoured, must necessarily derive great advantage from the treaty. Those merchants and manufacturers enjoy a sort of monopoly in the country which is so indulgent to them. That country becomes a market both more extensive and more advantageous for their goods: more extensive, because the goods of other nations being either excluded or subjected to heavier duties, it takes off a greater quantity of theirs: more advantageous, because the merchants of the favoured country, enjoying a sort of monopoly there, will often sell their goods for a better price than if exposed to the free competition of all other nations.

Such treaties, however, though they may be advantageous to the merchants and manufacturers of the favoured, are necessarily disadvantageous to those of the favouring country. A monopoly is thus granted against them to a foreign nation; and they must frequently buy the foreign goods they have occasion for, dearer than if the free competition of other nations was admitted.[15]

Smith's position on a public policy that was designed to comfort one sector of the economy at the expense of another can be summed up in the following sentence:

> To hurt in any degree the interest of any one order of citizens, for no other purpose but to promote that of some other, is evidently contrary to that justice and equality of treatment which the sovereign owes to all the different orders of his subjects.[16]

## *HARMONY OF INTERESTS*

Unlike the mercantilists who believed the gain of one person necessitated loss to another, Smith stressed the mutual benefits of exchange and a harmony of interests. Smith believed that when people were allowed to pursue their own interests, both the individual and society would benefit.

> Every individual is continually exerting himself to find out the most advantageous employment for whatever capital he can command. It is his own advantage, indeed, and not that of the society which he has in view. But the study of his own advantage naturally, or rather necessarily leads him to prefer that employment which is most advantageous to the society.[17]

> . . . every individual necessarily labours to render the annual revenue of the society as great as he can. He generally, indeed, neither intends to promote the public interest, nor knows how much he is promoting it. By preferring the support of domestic to that of foreign industry, he intends only his own security; and by directing that industry in such a manner as its produce may be of the greatest value, he intends only his own gain, and he is in this, as in many other cases, led by an invisible hand to promote

an end which was no part of his intention. Nor is it always the worse for the society that it was no part of it. By pursuing his own interest he frequently promotes that of the society more effectually than when he really intends to promote it. I have never known much good done by those who affected to trade for the public good. It is an affection, indeed, not very common among merchants, and very few words need be employed in dissuading them from it.[18]

It is competition that is Smith's invisible hand, and it is this which channels self-interest into socially desirable endeavors. A harmony of interests prevails in a free market system in the sense that survival is insured only if one produces the things that others want to buy.

Again, contrary to the tenets of mercantilism, Smith believed this harmony extended to trade among nations.

By such maxims as these, however, nations have been taught that their interest consisted in beggaring all their neighbours. Each nation has been made to look with an invidious eye upon the prosperity of all the nations with which it trades, and to consider their gain as its own loss. Commerce, which ought naturally to be, among nations, as among individuals, a bond of union and friendship, has become the most fertile source of discord and animosity. The capricious ambition of kings and ministers has not, during the present and the preceding century, been more fatal to the repose of Europe, than the impertinent jealousy of merchants and manufacturers. The violence and injustice of the rulers of mankind is an ancient evil, for which, I am afraid, the nature of human affairs can scarce admit of a remedy. But the mean rapacity, the monopolizing spirit of merchants and manufacturers, who neither are, nor ought to be, the rulers of mankind, though it cannot perhaps be corrected, may very easily be prevented from disturbing the tranquillity of any body but themselves.

That it was the spirit of monopoly which originally both invented and propagated this doctrine, cannot be doubted; and they who first taught it were by no means such fools as they who believed it. In every country it always is and must be the interest of the great body of the people to buy whatever they want of those who sell it cheapest. The proposition is so very manifest, that it seems ridiculous to take any pains to prove it; nor could it ever have been called in question, had not the interested sophistry of merchants and manufacturers confounded the common sense of mankind.

Their interest is, in this respect, directly opposite to that of the great body of the people. As it is the interest of the freemen of a corporation to hinder the rest of the inhabitants from employing any workmen but themselves, so it is the interest of the merchants and manufacturers of every country to secure to themselves the monopoly of the home market. Hence in Great Britain, and in most other European countries, the extraordinary duties upon almost all goods imported by alien merchants. Hence the high duties and prohibitions upon all those foreign manufactures which can come into competition with our own. Hence too the extraordinary restraints upon the importation of almost all sorts of goods from those countries with which the balance of trade is supposed to be disadvantageous; that is, from those against whom national animosity happens to be most violently inflamed.

The wealth of a neighbouring nation, however, though dangerous in war and politics, is certainly advantageous in trade. In a state of hostility it may enable our enemies to maintain fleets and armies superior to our own; but in a state of peace and commerce it must likewise enable them to exchange with us to a greater value, and to afford a better market, either for the immediate produce of our own industry, or for whatever is purchased with that produce. As a rich man is likely to be a better customer to the industrious people in his neigbbourhood, than a poor, so is likewise a rich nation. A rich man, indeed, who is himself a manufacturer, is a very dangerous neighbour to all those who deal in the same way. All the rest of the neighbourhood, however, by far the greatest number, profit by the good market which his expence affords them. They even profit by his underselling the poorer workmen who deal in the same way with him. The manufacturers of a rich nation, in the same manner, may no doubt be very dangerous rivals to those of their neighbours. This very competition, however, is advantageous to the great body of the people, who profit greatly besides by the good market which the great expence of such a nation affords them in every other way. Private people who want to make a fortune, never think of retiring to the remote and poor provinces of the country, but resort either to the capital, or to some of the great commercial towns. They know, that, where little wealth circulates, there is little to be got, but that where a great deal is in motion, some share of it may fall to them. The same maxims which would in this manner direct the common sense of one, or ten, or twenty individuals, should regulate the judgment of one, or ten, or twenty millions, and should make a whole nation regard the riches of its neighbours, as a probable cause and occasion for itself to acquire riches. A nation that would enrich itself by foreign trade, is certainly most likely to do so when its neighbours are all rich, industrious, and commercial nations.[19]

Smith challenged those who predicted disaster if free trade was established.

But the very same circumstances which would have rendered an open and free commerce between the two countries so advantageous to both, have occasioned the principal obstructions to that commerce. Being neighbours, they are necessarily enemies, and the wealth and power of each becomes, upon that account, more formidable to the other; and what would increase the advantage of national friendship, serves only to inflame the violence of national animosity. They are both rich and industrious nations; and the merchants and manufacturers of each, dread the competition of the skill and activity of those of the other. Mercantile jealousy is excited, and both inflames, and is itself inflamed, by the violence of national animosity: And the traders of both countries have announced, with all the passionate confidence of interested falsehood, the certain ruin of each, in consequence of that unfavourable balance of trade, which, they pretend, would be the infallible effect of an unrestrained commerce with the other.

There is no commercial country in Europe of which the approaching ruin has not frequently been foretold by the pretended doctors of this system, from an unfavourable balance of trade. After all the anxiety, however, which they have excited about this, after all the vain attempts of almost all trading nations to turn that balance in their own favour and against their neighbours, it does not appear that any one nation in Europe has been in any respect impoverished by this cause. Every town and country, on the contrary, in proportion as they have opened their ports to all nations, instead of being ruined by this free trade, as the principles of the commercial system would lead us to expect, have been enriched by it.[20]

# Chapter 6

## The Attack on Government

We already have seen Smith's hostility to particular laws. His disdain for government intervention also stemmed from a belief that private individuals made much better decisions than government officials. He found British colonial policy most discouraging.

### *MERCANTILISM*

What is the species of domestic industry which his capital can employ and of which the produce is likely to be of the greatest value, every individual, it is evident can, in his local situation, judge much better than any statesman or lawgiver can do for him. The statesman, who should attempt to direct private people in what manner they ought to employ their capitals, would not only load himself with a most unnecessary attention, but assume an authority which could safely be trusted, not only to no single person, but to no council or senate whatever, and which would no-where be so dangerous as in the hands of a man who had folly and presumption enough to fancy himself fit to exercise it.[1]

He has this to say about the East India Company:

It is a very singular government in which every member of the administration wishes to get out of the country, and consequently to have done with the government, as soon as he can, and to whose interest, the day after he has left it and carried his whole fortune with him, it is perfectly indifferent though the whole country was swallowed up by an earthquake.[2]

Smith's examination of the wool industry provides a good illustration of socially harmful legislation.

Our woollen manufacturers have been more successful than any other class of workmen, in persuading the legislature that the prosperity of the nation depended upon the success and extension of their particular business. They have not only obtained a monopoly against the consumers by an absolute prohibition of importing woollen cloths from any foreign country; but they have likewise obtained another monopoly against the sheep farmers and growers of wool, by a similar prohibition of the exportation of live sheep and wool. The severity of many of the laws which have been enacted for the security of the revenue is very justly complained of, as imposing heavy penalties upon actions which, antecedent to the statutes that declared them to be crimes, had always been understood to be innocent. But the cruellest of our revenue laws, I will venture to affirm, are mild and gentle, in comparison of some of those which the clamour of our merchants and manufacturers has extorted from the legislature, for the support of their own absurd and oppressive monopolies. Like the laws of Draco, these laws may be said to be all written in blood.[3]

Penalties for violating these laws included monetary fines, forfeiture of goods, imprisonment, amputation of the hand, and death. The following passages indicate the complexity of such regulations.

In order to prevent exportation, the whole inland commerce of wool is laid under very burdensome and oppressive restrictions. It cannot be packed in any box, barrel, cask, case, chest, or any other package, but only in packs of leather or pack-cloth, on which must be marked on the outside the words wool or yarn, in large letters not less than three inches long, on pain of forfeiting the same and the package, and three shillings for every pound weight, to be paid by the owner or packer. It cannot be loaden on any horse or cart, or carried by land within five miles of the coast, but between sun-rising and sun-setting, on pain of forfeiting the same, the horses and carriages. The hundred next adjoining to the sea coast, out of or through which the wool is carried or exported, forfeits twenty pounds, if the wool is under the value of ten pounds; and if of greater value, then treble that value, together with treble costs, to be sued for within the year. The execution to be against any two of the inhabitants, whom the sessions must reimburse, by an assessment on the other inhabitants, as in the cases of robbery. And if any person compounds with the hundred for less than this penalty, he is to be imprisoned for five years; and any other person may prosecute. These regulations take place through the whole kingdom.

But in the particular counties of Kent and Sussex the restrictions are still more troublesome. Every owner of wool within ten miles of the sea-coast must give an account in writing, three days after shearing, to the next officer of the customs, of the number of his fleeces, and of the places where they are lodged. And before he removes any part of them he must give the like notice of the number and weight of the fleeces, and of the name and abode of the person to whom they are sold, and of the place to which it is intended they should be carried. No person within fifteen miles of the sea, in the said counties, can buy any wool, before he enters into bond to the king, that no part of the wool which he shall so buy shall be sold by him to any other person within fifteen miles of the sea. If any wool is found carrying towards the sea-side in the said counties, unless it has been entered and security given as aforesaid, it is forfeited, and the offender also forfeits three shillings for every pound weight. If any person lays any wool, not entered as aforesaid, within fifteen miles of the sea, it must be seized and forfeited; and if, after such seizure, any person shall claim the same, he must give security to the Exchequer, that if he is cast upon trial he shall pay treble costs, besides all other penalties.

When such restrictions are imposed upon the inland trade, the coasting trade, we may believe, cannot be left very free. Every owner of wool who carrieth or causeth to be carried any wool to any port or place on the sea-coast, in order to be from thence transported by sea to any other place or port on the coast, must first cause an entry there of to be made at the port from whence it is intended to be conveyed, containing the weight, marks, and number of the packages before he brings the same within five miles of that port; on pain of forfeiting the same, and also the horses, carts, and other carriages; and also of suffering and forfeiting, as by the other laws in force against the exportation of wool.[4]

In another example, Smith argued that state policy rather than private avarice was likely to be the cause of a shortage.

Whoever examines, with attention, the history of the dearths and famines which have afflicted any part of Europe, during either the course of the present or that of the two preceding centuries, of several of which we have pretty exact accounts, will find, I believe, that a dearth never has arisen from any combination among the inland dealers in corn, nor from any other cause but a real scarcity, occasioned sometimes, perhaps, and in some particular places, by the waste of war, but in by far the greatest number of cases, by the fault of the seasons; and that a famine has never arisen from any other cause but the violence of government attempting, by improper means, to remedy the inconveniencies of a dearth.

In an extensive corn country, between all the different parts of which there is a free commerce and communication, the scarcity occasioned by the most unfavourable seasons can never be so great as to produce a famine; and the scantiest crop, if managed with frugality and oeconomy, will maintain, through the year, the same number of people that are commonly fed in a more affluent manner by one of the moderate plenty. The seasons most unfavourable to the crop are those of excessive drought or excessive rain. But, as corn grows equally upon high and low lands, upon grounds that are disposed to be too wet, and upon those that are disposed to be too dry, either the drought or the rain which is hurtful to one part of the country is favourable to another; and though both in the wet and in the dry season the crop is a good deal less than in one more properly tempered, yet in both what is lost in one part of the country is in some measure compensated by what is gained in the other. In rice countries, where the crop not only requires a very moist soil, but where in a certain period of its growing it must be laid under water, the effects of a drought are much more dismal. Even in such countries, however, the drought is, perhaps, scarce ever so universal, as necessarily to occasion a famine, if the government would allow a free trade. The drought in Bengal, a few years ago, might probably have occasioned a very great dearth. Some improper regulations, some injudicious restraints imposed by the servants of the East India Company upon the rice trade, contributed, perhaps, to turn that dearth into a famine.

When the government, in order to remedy the inconveniences of a dearth, orders all the dealers to sell their corn at what it supposes a reasonable price, it either hinders them from bringing it to market, which may sometimes produce a famine even in the beginning of the season; or if they bring it thither, it enables the people, and thereby encourages them to consume it so fast, as must necessarily produce a famine before the end of the season. The unlimited, unrestrained freedom of the corn trade, as it is the only effectual preventative of the miseries of a famine, so it is the best palliative of the inconveniencies of a dearth; for the inconveniencies of a real scarcity cannot be remedied; they can only be palliated. No trade deserves more the full protection of the law, and no trade requires it so much; because no trade is so much exposed to popular odium.

In years of scarcity the inferior ranks of people impute their distress to the avarice of the corn merchant, who becomes the object of their hatred and indignation. Instead of making profit upon such occasions, therefore, he is often in danger of being utterly ruined, and of having his magazines plundered and destroyed by their violence. It is in years of scarcity, however, when prices are high, that the corn merchant expects to make his principal profit. He is generally in contract with some farmers to furnish him for a certain number of years with a certain quantity of corn at a certain price. This contract price is settled according to what is supposed to be the moderate and reasonable, that is, the ordinary or average price, which, before the late years of scarcity, was commonly about eight-and-twenty shillings for the quarter of wheat, and for that of other grain in proportion. In years of scarcity, therefore, the corn merchant buys a great part of his corn for the ordinary price, and sells it for a much higher. That this extraordinary profit, however, is no more than sufficient to put his trade upon a fair level with other trades, and to compensate the many losses which he sustains upon other occasions, both from the perishable nature of the commodity itself, and from the frequent and unforeseen fluctuations of its price, seems evident enough, from this single circumstance, that great fortunes are as seldom made in this as in any other trade. he popular odium, however, which attends it in years of scarcity, the only years in which it can be very profitable, renders people of character and fortune averse to enter into it. It is abandoned to an inferior set of dealers; and millers, bakers, mealmen, and meal factors, together with a number of

wretched hucksters, are almost the only middle people that, in the home market, come
between the grower and the consumer.[5]

Smith also provided insight as to why such laws
were passed.

The laws concerning corn may every where
be compared to the laws concerning religion.
The people feel themselves so much interested in what relates either to their subsistence in this life, or to their happiness in a
life to come, that government must yield to
their prejudices, and, in order to preserve
the public tranquillity, establish that system
which they approve of. It is upon this account, perhaps, that we so seldom find a
reasonable system established with regard
to either of those two capital objects.[6]

Smith portrayed government as wasteful, extravagant and unproductive. He believed that these
characteristics, together with its unsound economic
policies, retarded economic development. However,
he also thought that individuals following their own
interests would find ways to surmount such obstacles and sustain progress.

Great nations are never impoverished by
private, though they sometimes are by public prodigality and misconduct. The whole,

or almost the whole public revenue, is in
most countries employed in maintaining unproductive hands. Such are the people who
compose a numerous and splendid court, a
great ecclesiastical establishment, great
fleets and armies, who in time of peace produce nothing, and in time of war acquire
nothing which can compensate the expence
of maintaining them, even while the war
lasts. Such people, as they themselves produce nothing, are all maintained by the produce of other men's labour. When
multiplied, therefore, to an unnecessary
number, they may in a particular year consume so great a share of this produce, as
not to leave a sufficiency for maintaining
the productive labourers, who should repro-
duce it next year. The next year's produce,
therefore, will be less than that of the foregoing, and if the same disorder should continue, that of the third year will be still less
than that of the second. Those unproductive
hands, who should be maintained by a part
only of the spare revenue of the people, may
consume so great a share of their whole revenue, and thereby oblige so great a number
to encroach upon their capitals, upon the
funds destined for the maintenance of productive labour, that all the frugality and
good conduct of individuals may not be able
to compensate the waste and degradation of

produce occasioned by this violent and forced encroachment.

This frugality and good conduct, however, is upon most occasions, it appears from experience, sufficient to compensate, not only the private prodigality and misconduct of individuals, but the public extravagance of government. The uniform, constant, and uninterrupted effort of every man to better his condition, the principle from which public and national, as well as private opulence is originally derived, is frequently powerful enough to maintain the natural progress of things toward improvement, in spite both of the extravagance of government, and of the greatest errors of administration. Like the unknown principle of animal life, it frequently restores health and vigour to the constitution, in spite, not only of the disease, but of the absurd prescriptions of the doctor.[7]

But though the profusion of government must, undoubtedly, have retarded the natural progress of England towards wealth and improvement, it has not been able to stop it. The annual produce of its land and labour is, undoubtedly, much greater at present than it was either at the restoration or at the revolution. The capital, therefore, annually employed in cultivating this land, and in maintaining this labour, must likewise be much greater. In the midst of all the exactions of government, this capital has been silently and gradually accumulated by the private frugality and good conduct of individuals, by their universal, continual, and uninterrupted effort to better their own condition. It is this effort, protected by law and allowed by liberty to exert itself in the manner that is most advantageous, which has maintained the progress of England towards opulence and improvement in almost all former times, and which, it is to be hoped, will do so in all future times. England, however, as it has never been blessed with a very parsimonious government, so parsimony has at no time been the characteristical virtue of its inhabitants. It is the highest impertinence and presumption, therefore, in kings and ministers, to pretend to watch over the oeconomy of private people, and to restrain their expence, either by sumptuary laws, or by prohibiting the importation of foreign luxuries. They are themselves always, and without any exception, the greatest spendthrifts in the society. Let them look well after their own expence, and they may safely trust private people with theirs. If their own extravagance does not ruin the state, that of their subjects never will.[8]

Chapter 6

# THE COLONIES

Unhappy with the imperialistic aspects of mercantilism, Smith's displeasure was especially evident when he considered the motives for colonization.

The policy of Europe, therefore, has very little to boast of, either in the original establishment, or, so far as concerns their internal government, in the subsequent prosperity of the colonies of America.

Folly and injustice seem to have been the principles which presided over and directed the first project of establishing those colonies; the folly of hunting after gold and silver mines, and the injustice of coveting the possession of a country whose harmless natives, far from having ever injured the people of Europe, had received the first adventurers with every mark of kindness and hospitality.

The adventurers, indeed, who formed some of the later establishments, joined, to the chimerical project of finding gold and silver mines, other motives more reasonable and more laudable; but even these motives do very little honour to the policy of Europe.

The English puritans, restrained at home, fled for freedom to America, and established there the four governments of New England. The English catholics, treated with much greater injustice, established that of Maryland; the Quakers, that of Pennsylvania. The Portuguese Jews, persecuted by the inquisition, stript of their fortunes, and banished to Brazil, introduced, by their examples some sort of order and industry among the transported felons and strumpets, by whom that colony was originally peopled, and taught them the culture of the sugarcane. Upon all these different occasions it was, not the wisdom and policy, but the disorder and injustice of the European governments, which peopled and cultivated America.[9]

He contended that the monopoly privileges enjoyed by British merchants in America were harmful to the British economy and quite difficult to remove.

The monopoly of the colony trade besides, by forcing towards it a much greater proportion of the capital of Great Britain than what would naturally have gone to it, seems to have broken altogether that natural balance which would otherwise have taken place among all the different branches of British industry. The industry of Great Britain, instead of being accommodated to a great number of small markets, has been principally suited to one great market. Her commerce, instead of running in a great number of small channels, has been taught to run principally in one great channel. But the whole system of her industry and commerce has thereby been rendered less secure; the whole state of her body politic less healthful, than it otherwise would have been. In her present condition, Great Britain resembles one of those unwholesome bodies in which some of the vital parts are overgrown, and which, upon that account, are liable to many dangerous disorders scarce incident to those in which all the parts are more properly proportioned. A small stop in that great blood-vessel, which has been artificially swelled beyond its natural dimensions, and through which an unnatural proportion of the industry and commerce of the country has been forced to circulate, is very likely to bring on the most dangerous disorders upon the whole body politic. The expectation of a rupture with the colonies, accordingly, has struck the people of Great Britain with more terror than they ever felt for a Spanish armada, or a French invasion. It was this terror, whether well or ill grounded, which rendered the repeal of the stamp act, among the merchants at least, a popular measure. In the total exclusion from the colony market, was it to last only for a few years, the greater part of our merchants used to fancy that they foresaw an entire stop to their trade; the greater part of our master manufacturers, the entire ruin of their business; and the greater part of our workmen, an end of their employment. A rupture with any of our neighbours upon the continent, though likely too to occasion some stop or interruption in the employments of some of all these different orders of people, is foreseen, however, without any such general emotion. The blood, of which the circulation is stopt in some of the smaller vessels, easily disgorges itself into the greaters without occasioning any dangerous disorder; but, when it is stopt in any of the greater vessels, convulsions, apoplexy, or death, are the immediate and unavoidable consequences. If but one of those overgrown manufactures, which by means either of bounties or of the monopoly of the home and colony markets, have been artificially raised up to an unnatural height, finds some small stop or interruption in its employment, it frequently occasions a mutiny and disorder alarming to government, and embarrassing even to the deliberations of the legislature. How great, therefore, would be the disorder and confusion, it was thought, which must necessarily be occasioned by a sudden and entire stop in the employment of so great a proportion of our principal manufacturers?

Some moderate and gradual relaxation of the laws which give to Great Britain the exclusive trade to the colonies, till it is rendered in a great measure free, seems to be the only expedient which can, in all future times, deliver her from this danger, which can enable her or even force her to withdraw some part of her capital from this overgrown employment, and to turn it, though with less profit, towards other employments; and which, by gradually diminishing one branch of her industry and gradually increasing all the rest, can by degrees restore all the different branches of it to that natural, healthful, and proper proportion which perfect liberty necessarily establishes, and which perfect liberty can alone preserve. To open the colony trade all at once to all nations, might not only occasion some transitory inconveniency, but a great permanent loss to the greater part of those whose industry or capital is at present engaged in it. The sudden loss of the employment even of  the ships which import the eighty-two thousand hogsheads of tobacco, which are over and above the consumption of Great Britain, might alone be felt very sensibly. Such are the unfortunate effects of all the regulations of the mercantile system! They not only introduce very dangerous disorders into the state of body politic, but disorders which it is often difficult to remedy, without occasioning, for a time at least, still greater disorders.[10]

Smith believed that these harmful colonial policies reflected the interests of business.

To found a great empire for the sole purpose of raising up a people of customers, may at first sight appear a project fit only for a nation of shop-keepers. It is, however, a project altogether unfit for a nation of shopkeepers; but extremely fit for a nation whose government is influenced by shopkeepers. Such statesmen, and such statesmen only, are capable of fancying that they will find some advantage in employing the blood and treasure of their fellow-citizens, to found and maintain such an empire. Say to a shopkeeper, Buy me a good estate, and I shall always buy my clothes at your shop, even though I should pay somewhat dearer than what I can have them for at other shops; and you will not find him very forward to embrace your proposal. But should any other person buy you such an estate, the shopkeeper would be much obliged to your benefactor if he would enjoin you to buy all your clothes at his shop. England purchased for some of her subjects, who found themselves uneasy at home, a great estate in a distant country.[11]

But in the system of laws which has been established for the management of our American and West Indian colonies, the interest of the home-consumer has been sacrificed to that of the producer with a more extravagant profusion than in all our other commercial regulations. A great empire has been established for the sole purpose of raising up a nation of customers who should be obliged to buy from the shops of our different producers, all the goods with which these could supply them. For the sake of that little enhancement of price which this monopoly might afford our producers, the home-consumers have been burdened with the whole expence of maintaining and defending that empire. For this purpose, and for this purpose only, in the two last wars, more than two hundred millions have been spent, and a new debt of more than a hundred and seventy millions has been contracted over and above all that had been expended for the same purpose in former wars. The interest of this debt alone is not only greater than the whole extraordinary profit, which, it ever could be pretended, was made by the monopoly of the colony trade, but than the whole value of that

trade, or than the whole value of the goods,
which at an average have been annually exported to the colonies.

It cannot be very difficult to determine
who have been the contrivers of this whole
mercantile system; not the consumers, we
may believe, whose interest has been entirely neglected; but the producers, whose
interest has been so carefully attended to;
and among this latter class our merchants
and manufacturers have been by far the
principal architects. In the mercantile regulations, which have been taken notice of
in this chapter, the interest of our manufacturers has been most peculiarly attended to;
and the interest, not so much of the consumers, as that of some other sets of producers, has been sacrificed to it.[12]

Like his fellow countrymen, Adam Smith was
quite anxious about the problems overseas. He was
not at all sanguine about British victory over the
rebellious Americans.

They are very weak who flatter themselves
that, in the state to which things have come,
our colonies will be easily conquered by force
alone. The persons who now govern the res-
olutions of what they call their continental
congress, feel in themselves at this moment
a degree of importance which, perhaps, the

greatest subjects in Europe scarce feel. From shop-keepers, tradesmen, and attornies, they are become statesmen and legislators, and are employed in contriving a new form of government for an extensive empire, which, they flatter themselves, will become, and which, indeed, seems very likely to become, one of the greatest and most formidable that ever was in the world. Five hundred different people, perhaps, who in different ways act immediately under the continental congress; and five hundred thousand, perhaps, who act under those five hundred, all feel in the same manner a proportionable rise in their own importance. Almost every individual of the governing party in America, fills, at present in his own fancy, a station superior, not only to what he had ever filled before, but to what he had ever expected to fill; and unless some new object of ambition is presented either to him or to his leaders, if he has the ordinary spirit of a man, he will die in defence of that station. [13]

Although he thought it unlikely to occur, Smith even proposed that Britain voluntarily give up its power over the American colonies.

To propose that Great Britain should voluntarily give up all authority over her colonies, and leave them to elect their own magistrates, to enact their own laws, and to make peace and war as they might think proper, would be to propose such a measure as never was, and never will be adopted, by any nation in the world. No nation ever voluntarily gave up the dominion of any province, how troublesome soever it might be to govern it, and how small soever the revenue which it afforded might be in proportion to the expence which it occasioned. Such sacrifices, though they might frequently be agreeable to the interest, are always mortifying to the pride of every nation, and what is perhaps of still greater consequence, they are always contrary to the private interest of the governing part of it, who would thereby be deprived of the disposal of many places of trust and profit, of many opportunities of acquiring wealth and distinction, which the possession of the most turbulent, and, to the great body of the people, the most unprofitable province seldom fails to afford. The most visionary enthusiast would scarce be capable of proposing such a measure, with any serious hopes at least of its ever being adopted. If it was adopted, however, Great Britain would not only be immediately freed from the whole annual expence of the peace establishment of the colonies, but might settle with them such a treaty of commerce as would effectually secure to her a free trade, more advantageous to the great body of the people, though less so to the merchants, than the monopoly which she at present enjoys. By thus parting good friends, the natural affection of the colonies to the mother country, which, perhaps, our late dissensions have well nigh extinguished, would quickly revive. It might dispose them not only to respect, for whole centuries together, that treaty of  commerce which they had concluded with us at parting, but to favour us in war as well as in trade, and, instead of turbulent and factious subjects, to become our most faithful, affectionate, and generous allies; and the same sort of parental affection on the one side, and filial respect on the other, might revive between Great Britain and her colonies, which used to subsist between those of ancient Greece and the mother city from which they descended.[14]

Smith was of the opinion that it would be helpful if the colonies were represented in British Parliament in proportion to the tax revenue which they contributed to the British empire. Aware that such a proposal would generate fear on both sides of the Atlantic, he sought to assauge the anxiety of each party. He even offered the possibility that, one day, the capital of the entire empire might be found in America!

We, on this side the water, are afraid lest
the multitude of American representatives
should overturn the balance of the constitution, and increase too much either the influence of the crown on the one hand, or the
force of the democracy on the other. But if
the number of American representatives
were to be in proportion to the produce of
American taxation, the number of people to
be managed would increase exactly in proportion to the means of managing them; and
the means of managing, to the number of
people to be managed. The monarchical and
democratical parts of the constitution
would, after the union, stand exactly in the
same degree of relative force with regard to
one another as they had done before.

The people on the other side of the water
are afraid lest their distance from the seat
of government might expose them to many
oppressions. But their representatives in
parliament, of which the number ought from
the first to be considerable, would easily be
able to protect them from all oppression. The
distance could not much weaken the dependency of the representative upon the constit-
uent, and the former would still feel that he
owed his seat in parliament, and all the consequence which he derived from it, to the
good-will of the latter. It would be the interest of the former, therefore, to cultivate that

good-will by complaining, with all the authority of a member of the legislature, of
every outrage which any civil or military officer might be guilty of in those remote
parts of the empire. The distance of America
from the seat of government, besides, the
natives of that country might flatter themselves, with some appearance of reason too,
would not be of very long continuance. Such
has hitherto been the rapid progress of that
country in wealth, population and improvement, that in the course of little more than
a century, perhaps, the produce of American
might exceed that of British taxation. The
seat of the empire would then naturally remove itself to that part of the empire which
contributed most to the general defence and
support of the whole.[15]

That Smith was deeply worried about the deteri-
oration in the relationship of Britain to its colonies
is evident when he comes back to this subject at
the end of his book. He did think that it was proper
for Britain to ask the colonies to contribute to their
own defense. However, if they refused to do so, he
did not believe it was worth the cost to hold on to
them. These are the last words contained in *The
Wealth of Nations*:

It was because the colonies were supposed
to be provinces of the British empire, that

this expence was laid out upon them. But
countries which contribute neither revenue
nor military force towards the support of the
empire, cannot be considered as provinces.
They may perhaps be considered as append-
ages, as a sort of splendid and showy equipage of the empire. But if the empire can
no longer support the expence of keeping up
this equipage, it ought certainly to lay it
down; and if it cannot raise its revenue in
proportion to its expence, it ought, at least,
to accommodate its expence to its revenue.
If the colonies, notwithstanding their re-
fusal to submit to British taxes, are still to
be considered as provinces of the British
empire, their defence in some future war
may cost Great Britain as great an expence
as it ever has done in any former war. The
rulers of Great Britain have, for more than
a century past, amused the people with the
imagination that they possessed a great empire on the west side of the Atlantic. This
empire, however, has hitherto existed in
imagination only. It has hitherto been, not
an empire, but the project of an empire; not
a gold mine, but the project of a gold mine;
a project which has cost, which continues to
cost, and which, if pursued in the same way
as it has been hitherto, is likely to cost im-
mense expence, without being likely to bring
any profit; for the effects of the monopoly of

the colony trade, it has been shewn, are, to
the great body of the people, mere loss instead of profit. It is surely now time that
our rulers should either realize this golden
dream, in which they have been indulging
themselves, perhaps, as well as the people;
or, that they should awake from it themselves, and endeavour to awaken the people.
If the project cannot be completed, it ought
to be given up. If any of the provinces of
the British empire cannot be made to contribute towards the support of the whole
empire, it is surely time that Great Britain
should free herself from the expence of defending those provinces in time of war, and
of supporting any part of their civil or military establishments in time of peace, and
endeavour to accommodate her future views
and designs to the real mediocrity of her
circumstances.[16]

# Chapter 7

## The Proper Role of Government

Smith certainly was not one who believed that all government should be abolished. Rather he wished it to have a vital but restricted role. He showed insight into the structure of a sound tax system and was quite wary of government borrowing.

### *Functions of the State*

All systems either of preference or of restraint, therefore, being thus completely taken away, the obvious and simple system of natural liberty establishes itself of its own accord. Every man, as long as he does not violate the laws of justice, is left perfectly free to pursue his own interest his own way, and to bring both his industry and capital into competition with those of any other man, or order of men. The sovereign is completely discharged from a duty, in the attempting to perform which he must always be exposed to innumerable delusions, and for the proper performance of which no human wisdom or knowledge could ever be sufficient; the duty of superintending the industry of private people, and of directing it towards the employments most suitable to the interest of the society. According to the system of natural liberty, the sovereign has only three duties to attend to; three duties of great importance, indeed, but plain and intelligible to common understandings: first, the duty of protecting the society from the violence and invasion of other independent societies; secondly, the duty of protecting, as far as possible, every member of the society from the injustice or oppression of every other member of it, or the duty of establishing an exact administration of justice; and, thirdly, the duty of erecting and maintaining certain public works and certain public institutions, which it can never be for the interest of any individual, or small number of individuals, to erect and maintain; because the profit could never repay the expence to any individual or small number of individuals, though it may frequently do much more than repay it to a great society.[1]

Smith noted that there were different methods of providing for national defense.

The first duty of the sovereign, that of protecting the society from the violence and invasion of other independent societies, can be performed only by means of a military force. But the expence both of preparing this military force in time of peace, and of employing it in time of war, is very different in the different states of society, in the different periods of improvement.[2]

A shepherd has a great deal of leisure; a husbandman, in the rude state of husbandry, has some; and artificer or manufacturer has none at all. The first may, without any loss, employ a great deal of his time in martial exercises; the second may employ some part of it; but the last cannot employ a single hour in them without some loss, and his attention to his own interest naturally leads him to neglect them altogether. Those improvements in husbandry too, which the progress of arts and manufactures necessarily introduces, leave the husbandman as little leisure as the artificer. Military exercises come to be as much neglected by the inhabitants of the country as by those of the town, and the great body of the people becomes altogether unwarlike. That wealth, at the same time, which always follows the improvements of agriculture and manufactures, and which in reality is no more than the accumulated produce of those improvements, provokes the invasion of all their neighbours. An industrious, and upon that account a wealthy nation, is of all nations the most likely to be attacked; and unless the state takes some new measures for the public defence, the natural habits of the people render them altogether incapable of defending themselves.

In these circumstances, there seem to be but two methods, by which the state can make any tolerable provision for the public defence.

It may either, first, by means of a very rigorous police, and in spite of the whole bent of the interest, genius and inclinations of the people, enforce the practice of military exercises, and oblige either all the citizens of the military age, or a certain number of them, to join in some measure the trade of a soldier to whatever other trade or profession they may happen to carry on.

Or, secondly, by maintaining and employing a certain number of citizens in the constant practice of military exercises, it may render the trade of a soldier a particular trade, separate and distinct from all others.[3]

Smith preferred a standing army and felt it did not necessarily pose a threat to liberty. He also observed that national defense became more expensive as the art of warfare changed.

A well-regulated standing army is superior to every militia. Such an army, as it can best be maintained by an opulent and civilized nation, so it can alone defend such a nation against the invasion of a poor and barbarous neighbour. It is only by means of a standing army, therefore, that the civilization of any country can be perpetuated, or even preserved for any considerable time.

As it is only by means of a well-regulated standing army that a civilized country can be defended; so it is only by means of it, that a barbarous country can be suddenly and tolerably civilized. A standing army establishes, with an irresistible force, the law of the sovereign through the remotest provinces of the empire, and maintains some degree of regular government in countries which could not otherwise admit of any. Whoever examines, with attention, the improvements which Peter the Great introduced into the Russian empire, will find that they almost all resolve themselves into the establishment of a well-regulated standing army. It is the instrument which executes and maintains all his other regulations. That degree of order and internal peace, which that empire has ever since enjoyed, is altogether owing to the influence of that army.

Men of republican principles have been jealous of a standing army as dangerous to liberty. It certainly is so, wherever the interest of the general and that of the principal officers are not necessarily connected with the support of the constitution of the state. The standing army of Caesar destroyed the

Roman republic. The standing army of Cromwel turned the long parliament out of doors. But where the sovereign is himself the general, and the principal nobility and gentry of the country the chief officers of the army; where the military force is placed under the command of those who have the greatest interest in the support of the civil authority, because they have themselves the greatest share of that authority, a standing army can never be dangerous to liberty. On the contrary, it may in some cases be favourable to liberty. The security which it gives to the sovereign renders unnecessary that troublesome jealousy, which, in some modern republics, seems to watch over the minutest actions, and to be at all times ready to disturb the peace of every citizen. Where the security of the magistrate, though supported by the principal people of the country, is endangered by every popular discontent; where a small tumult is capable of bringing about in a few hours a great revolution, the whole authority of government must be employed to suppress and punish every murmur and complaint against it. To a sovereign, on the contrary, who feels himself supported, not only by the natural aristocracy of the country, but by a well-regulated standing army, the rudest, the most groundless, and the most licentious remonstrances can give little disturbance. He can safely pardon or neglect them, and his consciousness of his own superiority naturally disposes him to do so. That degree of liberty which approaches to licentiousness can be tolerated only in countries where the sovereign is secured by a well-regulated standing army. It is in such countries only, that the public safety does not require, that the sovereign should be trusted with any discretionary power, for suppressing even the impertinent wantonness of this licentious liberty.

The first duty of the sovereign, therefore, that of defending the society from the violence and injustice of other independent societies, grows gradually more and more expensive, as the society advances in civilization. The military force of the society, which originally cost the sovereign no expence either in time of peace or in time of war, must, in the progress of improvement, first be maintained by him in time of war, and afterwards even in time of peace.

The great change introduced into the art of war by the invention of fire-arms, has enhanced still further both the expence of exercising and disciplining any particular number of soldiers in time of peace, and that of employing them in time of war. Both their arms and their ammunition are become more expensive. A musquet is a more expensive machine than a javelin or a bow and arrows; a cannon or a mortar than a balista or a catapulta. The powder, which is spent in a modern review, is lost irrecoverably, and occasions a very considerable expence. The javelins and arrows which were thrown or shot in an ancient one, could easily be picked up again, and were besides of very little value. The cannon and the mortar are, not only much dearer, but much heavier machines than the balists or catapulta, and require a greater expence, not only to prepare them for the field, but to carry them to it. As the superiority of the modern artillery too, over that of the ancients is very great; it has become much more difficult, and consequently much more expensive, to fortify a town so as to resist even for a few weeks the attack of that superior artillery. In modern times many different causes contribute to render the defence of the society more expensive. The unavoidable effects of the natural progress of improvement have, in this respect, been a good deal enhanced by a great revolution in the art of war, to which a mere accident, the invention of gunpowder, seems to have given occasion.

In modern war the great expence of firearms gives an evident advantage to the nation which can best afford that expence; and consequently, to an opulent and civilized, over a poor and barbarous nation. In ancient times the opulent and civilized found it difficult to defend themselves against the poor and barbarous nations. In modern times the poor and barbarous find it difficult to defend themselves against the opulent and civilized. The invention of fire-arms, an invention which at first sight appears to be so pernicious, is certainly favourable both to the permanency and to the extension of civilization.[4]

Smith next considered the administration of justice. Here also, he showed that its expense would vary with the state to which society had evolved.

The second duty of the sovereign, that of protecting, as far as possible, every member of the society from the injustice or oppression of every other member of it, or the duty of establishing an exact administration of justice requires too very different degrees of expence in the different periods of society.

Among nations of hunters, as there is scarce any property, or at least none that exceeds the value of two or three days labour; so there is seldom any established magistrate or any regular administration of justice. Men who have no property can injure one another only in their persons or reputations. But when one man kills,

wounds, beats, or defames another, though
he to whom the injury is done suffers, he
who does it receives no benefit. It is otherwise with the injuries to property. The benefit of the person who does the injury is of
ten equal to the loss of him who suffers it.
Envy, malice, or resentment, are the only
passions which can prompt one man to injure another in his person or reputation.
But the greater part of men are not very
frequently under the influence of those passions; and the very worst men are so only
occasionally. As their gratification too, how
agreeable soever it may be to certain characters, is not attended with any real or permanent advantage, it is in the greater part
of men commonly restrained by prudential
considerations. Men may live together in society with some tolerable degree of security,
though there is no civil magistrate to protect them from the injustice of those passions. But avarice and ambition in the rich,
in the poor the hatred of labour and the love
of present ease and enjoyment, are the passions which prompt to invade property, passions much more steady in their operation,
and much more universal in their influence.
Wherever there is great property, there is
great inequality. For one very rich man,
there must be at least five hundred poor,
and the affluence of the few supposes the

indigence of the many. The affluence of the rich excites the indignation of the poor, who are often both driven by want, and prompted by envy, to invade his possessions. It is only under the shelter of the civil magistrate that the owner of that valuable property, which is acquired by the labour of many years, or perhaps of many successive generations, can sleep a single night in security. He is at all times surrounded by unknown enemies, whom, though he never provoked, he can never appease, and from whose injustice he can be protected only by the powerful arm of the civil magistrate continually held up to chastise it. The acquisition of valuable and extensive property, therefore, necessarily requires the establishment of civil government. Where there is no property, or at least none that exceeds the value of two or three days labour, civil government is not so necessary.[5]

Smith propounded the idea that the judicial branch of government should be separated from the executive.

When the judicial is united to the executive power, it is scarce possible that justice should not frequently be sacrificed to, what is vulgarly called, politics. The persons entrusted with the great interests of the state,

may, even without any corrupt views, sometimes imagine it necessary to sacrifice to
those interests the rights of a private man.
But upon the impartial administration of
justice depends the liberty of every individual, the sense which he has of his own security. In order to make every individual
feel himself perfectly secure in the possession of every right which belongs to him, it
is not only necessary that the judicial
should be separated from the executive
power, but that it should be rendered as
much as possible independent of that power.
The judge should not be liable to be removed from his office according to the ca-
price of that power. The regular payment of
his salary should not depend upon the good-
will, or even upon the good oeconomy of that
power.[6]

The third general function of government was to
provide public works and institutions. It consisted
of several parts.

The third and last duty of the sovereign or
commonwealth is that of erecting and maintaining those public institutions and those
public works, which, though they may be in
the highest degree advantageous to a great
society, are, however, of such a nature, that
the profit could never repay the expence to

any individual or small number of individuals, and which it therefore cannot be expected that any individual or small number of individuals should erect or maintain.[7]

Public works served to facilitate a nation's commerce and included roads, bridges and harbors. Smith believed that they should be undertaken by local rather than national governments.

Even those public works which are of such a nature that they cannot afford any revenue for maintaining themselves, but of which the conveniency is nearly confined to some particular place or district, are always better maintained by a local or provincial administration, than by the general revenue of the state, of which the executive power must always have the management. Were the streets of London to be lighted and paved at the expence of the treasury, is there any probability that they would be so well lighted and paved as they are at present, or even at so small an expence? The expence, besides, instead of being raised by a local tax upon the inhabitants of each particular street, parish, or district in London, would, in this case, be defrayed out of the general revenue of the state, and would consequently be raised by a tax upon all the inhabitants of the kingdom, of whom the greater part derive no sort of benefit from the lighting and paving of the streets of London.

The abuses which sometimes creep into the local and provincial administration of a local and provincial revenue, how enormous soever they may appear, are in reality, however, almost always very trifling, in comparison of those which commonly take place in the administration and expenditure of the revenue of a great empire. They are, besides, much more easily corrected. Under the local or provincial administration of the justices of the peace in Great Britain, the six days labour which the country people are obliged to give to the reparation of the highways, is not always perhaps very judiciously applied, but it is scarce ever exacted with any circumstance of cruelty or oppression. In France, under the administration of the intendants, the application is not always more judicious, and the exaction is frequently the most cruel and oppressive. Such Corvees, as they are called, make one of the principal instruments of tyranny by which those officers chastise any parish or communeaute which has had the misfortune to fall under their displeasure.[8]

The establishment of educational institutions was a vital component of this third function. One reason for its importance was that the division of labor, that fount of economic progress, had unfortunate side effects.

In the progress of the division of labour, the employment of the far greater part of those who live by labour, that is, of the great body of the people, comes to be confined to a few very simple operations; frequently to one or two. But the understandings of the greater part of men are necessarily formed by their ordinary employments. The man whose whole life is spent in performing a few simple operations, of which the effects too are, perhaps, always the same, or very nearly the same, has no occasion to exert his understanding, or to exercise his invention in finding out expedients for removing difficulties which never occur. He naturally loses, therefore, the habit of such exertion, and generally becomes as stupid and ignorant as it is possible for a human creature to become. The torpor of his mind renders him, not only incapable of relishing or bearing a part in any rational conversation, but of conceiving any generous, noble, or tender sentiment, and consequently of forming any just judgment concerning many even of the ordinary duties of private life. Of the great and extensive interests of his country he is altogether incapable of judging; and unless very particular pains have been taken to render him otherwise, he is equally incapable of defending his country in war. The uniformity of his stationary life naturally corrupts the courage of his mind, and makes him regard with abhorrence the irregular, uncertain, and adventurous life of a soldier. It corrupts even the activity of his body, and renders him incapable of exerting his strength with vigour and perseverance, in any other employment than that to which he has been bred. His dexterity at his own particular trade seems, in this manner, to be acquired at the expence of his intellectual, social, and martial virtues. But in every improved and civilized society this is the state into which the labouring poor, that is, the great body of the people, must necessarily fall, unless government takes some pains to prevent it.[9]

According to Smith, there were social as well as individual benefits that accompanied education.

The same thing may be said of the gross ignorance and stupidity which, in a civilized society, seem so frequently to benumb the understandings of all the inferior ranks of people. A man without the proper use of the intellectual faculties of a man, is, if possible, more contemptible than even a coward, and seems to be mutilated and deformed in a still more essential part of the character of human nature. Though the state was to derive no advantage from the instruction of the inferior ranks of people, it would still deserve its attention that they should not be altogether uninstructed. The state, however, derives no inconsiderable advantage from their instruction. The more they are instructed, the less liable they are to the delusions of enthusiasm and superstition, which, among ignorant nations, frequently occasion the most dreadful disorders. An instructed and intelligent people besides, are always more decent and orderly than an ignorant and stupid one. They feel themselves, each individually, more respectable, and more likely to obtain the respect of their lawful superiors, and they are therefore more disposed to respect those superiors. They are more disposed to examine, and more capable of seeing through, the interested complaints of faction and sedition, and they are, upon that account, less apt to be misled into any wanton or unnecessary opposition to the measures of government. In free countries, where the safety of government depends very much upon the favourable judgment which the people may form of its conduct, it must surely be of the highest importance that they should not be disposed to judge rashly or capriciously concerning it.[10]

Smith was primarily concerned about the education of the common people rather than the upper classes and he suggested that it need not cost very much.

The education of the common people requires, perhaps, in a civilized and commercial society, the attention of the public more than that of people of some rank and fortune. People of some rank and fortune are generally eighteen or nineteen years of age before they enter upon that particular business, profession, or trade, by which they propose to distinguish themselves in the world. They have before that full time to acquire, or at least to fit themselves for afterwards acquiring, every accomplishment which can recommend them to the public esteem, or render them worthy of it. Their parents or guardians are generally sufficiently anxious that they should be so accomplished, and are, in most cases, willing enough to lay out the expence which is necessary for that purpose. If they are not always properly educated, it is seldom from the want of expence laid out upon their education; but from the improper application of that expence. It is seldom from the want of masters; but from the negligence and incapacity of the masters who are to be had, and from the difficulty, or rather from the impossibility which there is, in the present state of things, of finding any better. The employments too in which people of some rank or fortune spend the greater part of their lives, are not, like those of the common people, simple and uniform. They are almost all of them extremely complicated, and such as exercise the head more than the hands. The understandings of those who are engaged in such employments can seldom grow torpid for want of exercise. The employments of people of some rank and fortune, besides, are seldom such as harass them from morning to night. They generally have a good deal of leisure, during which they may perfect themselves in every branch either of useful or ornamental knowledge of which they may have laid the foundation, or for which they may have acquired some taste in the earlier part of life.

It is otherwise with the common people. They have little time to spare for education. Their parents can scarce afford to maintain them even in infancy. As soon as they are able to work, they must apply to some trade by which they can earn their subsistence. That trade too is generally so simple and uniform as to give little exercise to the understanding; while, at the same time, their labour is both so constant and so severe, that it leaves them little leisure and less inclination to apply to, or even to think of anything else.

But though the common people cannot, in any civilized society, be so well instructed as people of some rank and fortune, the most essential parts of education, however, to read, write, and account, can be acquired at so early a period of life, that the greater part even of those who are to be bred to the lowest occupations, have time to acquire them before they can be employed in those occupations. For a very small expence the public can facilitate, can encourage, and can even impose upon almost the whole body of the people, the necessity of acquiring those most essential parts of education.

The public can facilitate this acquisition by establishing in every parish or district a little school, where children may be taught for a reward so moderate, that even a common labourer may afford it; the master being partly, but not wholly paid by the public; because, if he was wholly, or even principally paid by it, he would soon learn to neglect his business. In Scotland the establishment of such parish schools has taught almost the whole common people to read, and a very great proportion of them to write and account. In England the establishment of charity schools has had an effect of the same kind, though not so universally, because the establishment is not so universal. If in those little schools the books, by which the children are taught to read, were a little more instructive than they commonly are; and if, instead of a little smattering of Latin, which the children of the common people are sometimes taught there, and which can scarce ever be of any use to them; they were instructed in the elementary parts of geometry and mechanics, the literary education of this rank of people would perhaps be as complete as it can be. There is scarce a common trade which does not afford some opportunities of applying to it the principles of geometry and mechanics, and which would not therefore gradually exercise and improve the common people in those principles, the necessary introduction to the most sublime as well as to the most useful sciences.[11]

It was Smith's belief that government should assist in the establishment of educational institutions while teachers ought to be paid by their students. This opinion, undoubtedly, reflected the poor teaching he encountered at Oxford. It also was consistent with his support for the incentives provided by competitive markets. The following passages illustrate his position.

In every profession, the exertion of the greater part of those who exercise it, is always in proportion to the necessity they are under of making that exertion. This necessity is greatest with those to whom the emoluments of their profession are the only source from which they expect their fortune, or even their ordinary revenue and subsistence. In order to acquire this fortune, or even to get this subsistence, they must, in the course of a year, execute a certain quantity of work of a known value; and, where the competition is free, the rivalship of competitors, who are all endeavouring to justle one another out of employment, obliges every man to endeavour to execute his work with a certain degree of exactness. The greatness of the objects which are to be acquired by success in some particular professions may, no doubt, sometimes animate the exertion of a few men of extraordinary spirit and ambition. Great objects, however, are evidently not necessary in order to occasion the greatest exertions. Rivalship and emulation render excellency, even in mean professions, an object of ambition, and frequently, occasion the very greatest exertions. Great objects, on the contrary, alone and unsupported by the necessity of application, have seldom been sufficient to occasion any considerable exertion. In England, success in the profession of the law leads to some very great objects of ambition; and yet how few men, born to easy fortunes, have ever in this country been eminent in that profession?

The endowments of schools and colleges have necessarily diminished more or less the necessity of application in the teachers. Their subsistence, so far as it arises from their salaries, is evidently derived from a fund altogether independent of their success and reputation in their particular professions.

In some universities the salary makes but a part, and frequently but a small part of the emoluments of the teacher, of which the greater part arises from the honoraries or fees of his pupils. The necessity of application, though always more or less diminished, is not in this case entirely taken away. Reputation in his profession is still of some importance to him, and he still has some dependency upon the affection, gratitude, and favourable report of those who have attended upon his instructions; and these favourable sentiments he is likely to gain in no way so well as by deserving them, that is by the abilities and diligence with which he discharges every part of his duty.

In other universities the teacher is prohibited from receiving any honorary or fee from his pupils, and his salary constitutes the whole of the revenue which he derives from his office. His interest is, in this case, set as directly in opposition to his duty as it is possible to set it. It is the interest of every man to live as much at his ease as he can; and if his emoluments are to be precisely the same, whether he does, or does not perform some very laborious duty, it is certainly his interest, at least as interest is vulgarly understood, either to neglect it altogether, or, if he is subject to some authority which will not suffer him to do this, to perform it in as careless and slovenly a manner as that authority will permit. If he is naturally active and a lover of labour, it is his interest to employ that activity in any way, from which he can derive some advantage, rather than in the performance of his duty, from which he can derive none.

If the authority to which he is subject resides in the body corporate, the college, or university, of which he himself is a member, and in which the greater part of the other members are, like himself, persons who either are, or ought to be teachers; they are likely to make a common cause, to be all very indulgent to one another, and every man to consent that his neighbour may neglect his duty, provided be himself is allowed to neglect his own. In the university of Oxford, the greater part of the public professors

have, for these many years, given up altogether even the pretence of teaching.

If the authority to which he is subject resides, not so much in the body corporate of
which he is a member, as in some other extraneous persons, in the bishop of the dio-
cese for example; in the governor of the
province; or, perhaps, in some minister of
state; it is not indeed in this case very likely
that he will be suffered to neglect his duty
altogether. All that such superiors, however,
can force him to do, is to attend upon his
pupils a certain number of hours, that is,
to give a certain number of lectures in the
week or in the year. What those lectures
shall be, must still depend upon the diligence of the teacher; and that diligence is
likely to be proportioned to the motives
which he has for exerting it. An extraneous
jurisdiction of this kind, besides, is liable to
be exercised both ignorantly and capriciously.
In its nature it is arbitrary and discretionary,
and the person who exercise it, neither attending upon the lectures of the teacher
themselves, nor perhaps, understanding the
sciences which it is his business to teach, are
seldom capable of exercising it with judgment. From the insolence of office too they
are frequently indifferent how they exercise
it, and are very apt to censure or deprive
him of his office wantonly, and without any

just cause. The person subject to such jurisdiction is necessarily degraded by it, and,
instead of being one of the most respectable,
is rendered one of the meanest and most
contemptible persons in the society. It is by
powerful protection only that he can effectually guard himself against the bad usage
to which he is at all times exposed; and this
protection he is most likely to gain, not by
ability or diligence in his profession, but by
obsequiousness to the will of his superiors,
and by being ready, at all times, to sacrifice
to that will the rights, the interest, and the
honour of the body corporate of which he is
a member. Whoever has attended for any
considerable time to the administration of
a French university, must have had occasion
to remark the effects which naturally result
from an arbitrary and extraneous jurisdiction of this kind.

Whatever forces a certain number of students to any college or university, independent of the merit or reputation of the
teachers, tends more or less to diminish the
necessity of that merit or reputation. The
privileges of graduates in arts, in law,
physic and divinity, when they can be obtained only by residing a certain number of
years in certain universities, necessarily
force a certain number of students to such
universities, independent of the merit or

reputation of the teachers.

The privileges of graduates are a sort of statutes of apprenticeship, which have contributed to the improvement of education, just as the other statutes of apprenticeship have to that of arts and manufactures.

The charitable foundations of scholarships, exhibitions, bursaries, &c. necessarily attach a certain number of students to certain colleges, independent altogether of the merit of those particular colleges. Were the students upon such charitable foundations left free to chuse what college they liked best, such liberty might perhaps contribute to excite some emulation among different colleges. A regulation, on the contrary, which prohibited even the independent members of every particular college from leaving it, and going to any other, without leave first asked and obtained of that which they meant to abandon, would tend very much to extinguish that emulation.

If in each college the tutor or teacher, who was to instruct each student in all arts and sciences, should not be voluntarily chosen by the student, but appointed by the head of the college; and if, in case of neglect, inability, or bad usage, the student should not be allowed to change him for another, without leave first asked and obtained; such a regulation would not only tend very much to extinguish all emulation among the different tutors of the same college, but to diminish very much in all of them the necessity of diligence and of attention to their respective pupils. Such teachers, though very well paid by their students, might be as much disposed to neglect them as those who are not paid by them at all, or who have no other recompence but their salary.

If the teacher happens to be a man of sense, it must be an unpleasant thing to him to be conscious, while he is lecturing his students, that he is either speaking or reading nonsense, or what is very little better than nonsense. It must too be unpleasant to him to observe that the greater part of his students desert his lectures; or perhaps attend upon them with plain enough marks of neglect, contempt, and derision. If he is obliged, therefore, to give a certain number of lectures, these motives alone, without any other interest, might dispose him to take some pains to give tolerably good ones. Several different expedients, however may be fallen upon, which will effectually blunt the edge of all those incitements to diligence. The teacher, instead of explaining to his pupils himself the science in which he proposes to instruct them, may read some book upon it; and if this book is written in a foreign and dead language, by interpreting it to them into their own; or, what would give him still less trouble, by making them interpret it to him, and by now and then making an occasional remark upon it, he may flatter himself that he is giving a lecture. The slightest degree of knowledge and application will enable him to do this, without exposing himself to contempt or derision, or saying any thing that is really foolish, absurd, or ridiculous. The discipline of the college, at the same time, may enable him to force all his pupils to the most regular attendance upon this sham-lecture, and to maintain the most decent and respectful behaviour during the whole time of performance.

The discipline of colleges and universities is in general contrived, not for the benefit of the students, but for the interest, or more properly speaking, for the ease of the masters. Its object is, in all cases, to maintain the authority of the master, and whether he neglects or performs his duty, to oblige the students, in all cases to behave to him as if he performed it with the greatest diligence and ability. It seems to presume perfect wisdom and virtue in the one order, and the greatest weakness and folly in the other. Where the masters, however, really perform their duty, there are no examples, I believe, that the greater part of the students ever neglect theirs. No discipline is ever requisite to force attendance upon lectures which are really worth the attending, as is well known wherever any such lectures are given. Force and restraint may, no doubt, be in some degree requisite in order to oblige children, or very young boys, to attend to those parts of education which it is thought necessary for them to acquire during that early period of life; but after twelve or thirteen years of age, provided the master does his duty, force or restraint can scarce ever be necessary to carry on any part of education. Such is the generosity of the greater part of young men, that, so far from being disposed to neglect or despise the instructions of their master, provided he shows some serious intention of being of use to them, they are generally inclined to pardon a great deal of incorrectness in the performance of his duty, and sometimes even to conceal from the public a good deal of gross negligence.

Those parts of education, it is to be observed, for the teaching of which there are no public institutions, are generally the best taught. When a young man goes to a fencing or a dancing school, he does not indeed always learn to fence or to dance very well; but he seldom fails of learning to fence or to dance. The good effects of the riding

school are not commonly so evident. The expence of a riding school is so great, that in
most places it is a public institution. The
three most essential parts of literary education, to read, write, and account, it still continues to be more common to acquire in
private than in public schools; and it very
seldom happens that any body fails of acquiring them to the degree in which it is
necessary to acquire them.

In England the public schools are much
less corrupted than the universities. In the
schools the youth are taught, or at least
may be taught, Greek and Latin; that is,
every thing which the masters pretend to
teach, or which it is expected, they should
teach. In the universities the youth neither
are taught, nor always can find any proper
means of being taught, the sciences, which
it is the business of those incorporated bodies to teach. The reward of the schoolmaster
in most cases depends principally, in some
cases almost entirely, upon the fees or honoraries of his scholars. Schools have no exclusive privileges. In order to obtain the
honours of graduation, it is not necessary
that a person should bring a certificate of
his having studied a certain number of
years at a public school. If upon examination he appears to understand what is
taught there, no questions are asked about

the place where he learnt it.

The parts of education which are commonly taught in universities, it may, perhaps, be said are not very well taught. But had it not been for those institutions they would not have been commonly taught at all, and both the individual and the public would have suffered a good deal from the want of those important parts of education.[12]

Smith was not very pleased with the practice of sending youngsters abroad to receive their education.

In England, it becomes every day more and more the custom to send young people to travel in foreign countries immediately upon their leaving school, and without sending them to any university. Our young people, it is said, generally return home much improved by their travels. A young man who goes abroad at seventeen or eighteen, and returns home at one and twenty, returns three or four years older than he was when he went abroad; and at that age it is very difficult not to improve a good deal in three or four years. In the course of his travels, he generally acquires some knowledge of one or two foreign languages; a knowledge, however, which is seldom sufficient to enable him either to speak or write them with propriety. In other respects, he commonly returns home more conceited, more unprincipled, more dissipated, and more incapable of any serious application either to study or to business, than he could well have become in so short a time, had he lived at home. By travelling so very young, by spending in the most frivolous dissipation the most precious years of his life, at a distance from the inspection and controul of his parents and relations, every useful habit, which the earlier parts of his education might have had some tendency to form in him, instead of being rivetted and confirmed, is almost necessarily either weakened or effaced. Nothing but the discredit into which the universities are allowing themselves to fall, could ever have brought into repute so very absurd a practice as that of travelling at this early period of life. By sending his son abroad, a father delivers himself, at least for some time, from so disagreeable an object as that of a son unemployed, neglected, and going to ruin before his eyes.[13]

# FINANCING GOVERNMENT: TAXATION

One device for financing government expenditures is that of charging a fee — economists today refer to it as a user fee — to those who most directly benefit from a particular service. Smith gave his support to this method in such areas as education and the use of turnpikes. Taxation, however, is a much more important source of public funds. Adam Smith's four maxims of a good tax system still can be found in textbooks on public finance.

> I. The subjects of every state ought to contribute towards the support of the government, as nearly as possible, in proportion to their respective abilities; that is, in proportion to the revenue which they respectively enjoy under the protection of the state. The expence of government to the individuals of a great nation, is like the expence of management to the joint tenants of a great estate, who are all obliged to contribute in proportion to their respective interests in the estate. In the observation or neglect of this maxim consists, what is called the equality or inequality of taxation.[14]

> II. The tax which each individual is bound to pay ought to be certain, and not arbitrary. The time of payment, the manner of payment, the quantity to be paid, ought all to

be clear and plain to the contributor, and to every other person. Where it is otherwise, every person subject to the tax is put more or less in the power of the tax-gatherer, who can either aggravate the tax upon any obnoxious contributor, or extort, by the terror of such aggravation, some present or perquisite to himself. The uncertainty of taxation encourages the insolence and favours the corruption of an order of men who are naturally unpopular, even where they are neither insolent nor corrupt. The certainty of what each individual ought to pay is, in taxation, a matter of so great importance, that a very considerable degree of inequality, it appears, I believe, from the experience of all nations, is not near so great an evil as a very small degree of uncertainty.

III. Every tax ought to be levied at the time, or in the manner, in which it is most likely to be convenient for the contributor to pay it.[15]

IV. Every tax ought to be so contrived as both to take out and to keep out of the pockets of the people as little as possible, over and above what it brings into the public treasury of the state. A tax may either take out or keep out of the pockets of the people a great deal more than it brings into the public treasury, in the four following ways.

First, the levying of it may require a great
number of officers, whose salaries may eat
up the greater part of the produce of the
tax, and whose perquisites may impose another additional tax upon the people. Secondly, it may obstruct the industry of the
people, and discourage them from applying
to certain branches of business which might
give maintenance and employment to great
multitudes. While it obliges the people to
pay, it may thus diminish, or perhaps destroy, some of the funds which might enable
them more easily to do so. Thirdly, by the
forfeitures and other penalties which those
unfortunate individuals incur who attempt
unsuccessfully to evade the tax, it may frequently ruin them, and thereby put an end
to the benefit which the community might
have received from the employment of their
capitals. An injudicious tax offers a great
temptation to smuggling. But the penalties
of smuggling must rise in proportion to the
temptation. The law, contrary to all the ordinary principles of justice, first creates the
temptation, and then punishes those who
yield to it; and it commonly enhances the
punishment too in proportion to the very
circumstance which ought certainly to alle-
viate it, the temptation to commit the crime.
Fourthly, by subjecting the people to the frequent visits and the odious examination of

the tax-gatherers, it may expose them to much unnecessary trouble, vexation, and oppression; and though vexation is not, strictly speaking, expence, it is certainly equivalent to the expence at which every man would be willing to redeem himself from it. It is in some one or other of these four different ways that taxes are frequently so much more burdensome to the people than they are beneficial to the sovereign.[16]

In matters of finance, as elsewhere, Smith is suspicious of government.

There is no art which one government sooner learns of another, than that of draining money from the pockets of the people.[17]

He contended that high taxes were counterproductive as revenue raisers and served to distort human behavior.

The high duties which have been imposed upon the importation of many different sorts of foreign goods, in order to discourage their consumption in Great Britain, have in many cases served only to encourage smuggling; and in all cases have reduced the revenue of the customs below what more moderate duties would have afforded. The saying of Dr. Swift, that in the arithmetic of the customs two and two, instead of making four, make some times only one, holds perfectly true with regard to such heavy duties, which never could have been imposed, had not the mercantile system taught us, in many cases, to employ taxation as an instrument, not of revenue, but of monopoly.[18]

. . . the hope of evading such taxes by smuggling gives frequent occasion to forfeitures and other penalties, which entirely ruin the smuggler; a person, who, though no doubt highly blameable for violating the laws of his country, is frequently incapable of violating those of natural justice, and would have been, in every respect, an excellent citizen, had not the laws of his country made that a crime which nature never meant to be so. In those corrupted governments where there is at least a general suspicion of much unnecessary expence, and great misapplication of the public revenue, the laws which guard it are little respected. Not many people are scrupulous about smuggling, when, without perjury, they can find any easy and safe opportunity of doing so. To pretend to have any scruple about buying smuggled goods, though a manifest encouragement to the violation of the revenue laws, and to the perjury which almost always attends it, would in most countries be regarded as one of those pedantic pieces of hypocrisy which, instead of gaining credit with any body, serve only to expose the person who affects to practise them, to the suspicion of being a greater knave than most of his neighbours. By this indulgence of the public, the smuggler is often encouraged to continue a trade which he is thus taught to consider as in some measure innocent; and when the severity of the revenue laws is ready to fall upon him, he is frequently disposed to defend with violence, what he has been accustomed to regard as his just property. From being at first, perhaps, rather imprudent than criminal, he at last too often becomes one of the hardiest and most determined violators of the laws of society. By the ruin of the smuggler, his capital, which had before been employed in maintaining productive labour, is absorbed either in the revenue of the state or in that of the revenue-officer, and is employed in maintaining unproductive, to the diminution of the general capital of the society, and of the useful industry which it might otherwise have maintained.[19]

Chapter 7

## FINANCING GOVERNMENT: BORROWING AND THE NATIONAL DEBT

Smith had much to say about borrowing and one point that he stressed was the importance of confidence as a basis for the extension of credit.

> Commerce and manufactures can seldom flourish long in any state which does not enjoy a regular administration of justice, in which the people do not feel themselves secure in the possession of their property, in which the faith of contracts is not supported by law, and in which the authority of the state is not supposed to be regularly employed in enforcing the payment of debts from all those who are able to pay. Commerce and manufactures, in short, can seldom flourish in any state in which there is not a certain degree of confidence in the justice of government. The same confidence which disposes great merchants and manufacturers, upon ordinary occasions, to trust their property to the protection of a particular government; disposes them, upon extraordinary occasions, to trust that government with the use of their property.[20]

He was pessimistic, indeed, about the effects of rising public debt among European nations.

> The progress of the enormous debts which at present oppress, and will in the long-run probably ruin, all the great nations of Europe, has been pretty uniform.[21]

Smith was very much aware that the short-term interests of the politician led him to prefer borrowing.

> To relieve the present exigency is always the object which principally interests those immediately concerned in the administration of public affairs. The future liberation of the public revenue, they leave to the care of posterity.[22]

He noted that one effect of using government borrowing to finance a war might be to extend the length of the conflict.

> It is only during the continuance of war, however, that the system of funding has this advantage over the other system. Were the expence of war to be defrayed always by a revenue raised within the year, the taxes from which that extraordinary revenue was drawn would last no longer than the war. The ability of private people to accumulate, though less during the war, would have been greater during the peace than under the system of funding. War would not necessarily have occasioned the destruction of

any old capitals, and peace would have occasioned the accumulation of many more
new. Wars would in general be more speed-
ily concluded, and less wantonly undertaken. The people feeling, during the
continuance of the war, the complete burden
of it, would soon grow weary of it, and government, in order to humour them, would
not be under the necessity of carrying it on
longer than it was necessary to do so. The
foresight of the heavy and unavoidable burdens of war would binder the people from
wantonly calling for it when there was no
real or solid interest to fight for.[23]

Smith had little use for those who justified government borrowing by saying we owe it to ourselves.

In the payment of the interest of the public
debt, it has been said, it is the right hand
which pays the left. The money does not go
out of the country. It is only a part of the
revenue of one set of the inhabitants which
is transferred to another; and the nation is
not a farthing the poorer. This apology is
founded altogether in the sophistry of the
mercantile system, and after the long examination which I have already bestowed upon
that system, it may perhaps be unnecessary
to say any thing further about it. It supposes, besides, that the whole public debt is

owing to the inhabitants of the country,
which happens not to be true; the Dutch, as
well as several other foreign nations, having
a very considerable share in our public
funds. But though the whole debt was owing
to the inhabitants of the country, it would
not upon that account be less pernicious.[24]

Smith was quite concerned that a large national
debt — Great Britain's was about one hundred
twenty-nine million pounds in 1775 — would lead
to bankruptcy.

When national debts have once been accumulated to a certain degree, there is scarce,
I believe, a single instance of their having
been fairly and completely paid. The liber-
ation of the public revenue, if it has ever
been brought about at all, has always been
brought about by a bankruptcy; sometimes
by an avowed one, but always by a real one,
though frequently by a pretended payment.
The raising of the denomination of the coin
has been the most usual expedient by which
a real public bankruptcy has been disguised
under the appearance of a pretended payment. If a sixpence, for example, should either by act of parliament or royal
proclamation be raised to the denomination
of a shilling, and twenty six-pences to that
of a pound sterling; the person who under

the old denomination had borrowed twenty shillings, or near four ounces of silver, would under the new, pay with twenty six-pences, or with something less than two ounces. A national debt of about a hundred and twenty-eight millions, nearly the capital of the funded and unfunded debt of Great Britain, might in this manner be paid with about sixty-four millions of our present money. It would indeed be a pretended payment only, and the creditors of the public would really be defrauded of ten shillings in the pound of what was due to them. The calamity too would extend much further than to the creditors of the public, and those of every private person would suffer a proportionable loss; and this without any advantage, but in most cases with a great additional loss, to the creditors of the public. If the creditors of the public indeed were generally much in debt to other people, they might in some measure compensate their loss by paying their creditors in the same coin in which the public had paid them. But in most countries the creditors of the public are, the greater part of them, wealthy people, who stand more in the relation of creditors than in that of debtors towards the rest of their fellow-citizens. A pretended payment of this kind, therefore, instead of alleviating, aggravates in most cases the loss of the creditors of the public; and without any advantage to the public, extends the calamity to a great number of other innocent people. It occasions a general and most pernicious subversion of the fortunes of private people; enriching in most cases the idle and profuse debtor at the expence of the industrious and frugal creditor, and transporting a great part of the national capital from the hands which were likely to increase and improve it, to those which are likely to dissipate and destroy it. When it becomes necessary for a state to declare itself bankrupt, in the same manner as when it becomes necessary for an individual to do so, a fair, open, and avowed bankruptcy is always the measure which is both least dishonourable to the debtor, and least hurtful to the creditor. The honour of a state is surely very poorly provided for, when, in order to cover the disgrace of a real bankruptcy, it has recourse to a juggling trick of this kind, so easily seen through, and to at the same time so extremely pernicious.[25]

# Chapter 8

## Champion of the Consumer

Although Smith was more concerned with economic growth than equality, the latter did not go unnoticed. He presented reasons for wage differentials and condemned the public policies that unjustifiably widened income inequalities. Often he is charged with being an apologist for business interests. Such an accusation, however, is far from the mark. In truth, Smith sympathized more with the worker than the master, but most of all with the consumer.

### *OCCUPATIONAL WAGE DIFFERENCES*

Although economic growth would cause the average level of wages to rise, it would not bring about equal wages for all. Smith showed that one source of wage differentials was based on the nature of different occupations. His analysis continues to be referred to in textbooks.

> The five following are the principal circumstances which, so far as I have been able to observe, make up for a small pecuniary gain in some employments, and counter-balance a great one in others; first, the agreeableness or disagreeableness of the employments themselves; secondly, the easiness and cheapness, or the difficulty and

expence of learning them; thirdly, the constancy or inconstancy of employment in them; fourthly, the small or great trust which must be reposed in those who exercise them; and fifthly, the probability or improbability of success in them.

First, The wages of labour vary with the ease or hardship, the cleanliness or dirtiness, the honourableness or dishonourableness of the employment. Thus in most places, take the year round, a journeyman taylor earns less than a journeyman weaver. His work is much easier. A journeyman weaver earns less than a journeyman smith. His work is not always easier, but it is much cleanlier. A journeyman blacksmith, though an artificer, seldom earns so much in twelve hours as a collier, who is only a labourer, does in eight. His work is not quite so dirty, is less dangerous, and is carried on in daylight, and above ground. Honour makes a great part of the reward of all honourable professions. In point of pecuniary gain, all things considered, they are generally under-recompensed, as I shall endeavour to show by and by. Disgrace has the contrary effect. The trade of a butcher is a brutal and an odious business; but it is in most places more profitable than the greater part of common trades. The most detestable of all employments, that of public executioner, is, in proportion to the quantity of work done, better paid than any common trade whatever.[1]

The second reason anticipated today's "human capital" approach of explaining wage differences.

Secondly, The wages of labour vary with the easiness and cheapness, or the difficulty and expence of learning the business.

When any expensive machine is erected, the extraordinary work to be performed by it before it is worn out, it must be expected, will replace the capital laid out upon it, with at least the ordinary profits. A man educated at the expence of much labour and time to any of those employments which require extraordinary dexterity and skill, may be compared to one of those expensive machines. The work which he learns to perform, it must be expected, over and above the usual wages of common labour, will replace to him the whole expence of his education, with at least the ordinary profits of an equally valuable capital. It must do this too in a reasonable time, regard being had to the very uncertain duration of human life, in the same manner as to the more certain duration of the machine.

The difference between the wages of skilled labour and those of common labour, is founded upon this principle.

The policy of Europe considers the labour of all mechanics, artificers, and manufacturers, as skilled labour; and that of all country labourers as common labour. It seems to suppose that of the former to be of a more nice and delicate nature than that of the later. It is so perhaps in some cases, but in the greater part it is quite otherwise, as I shall endeavour to shew by and by. The laws and customs of Europe, therefore, in order to qualify any person for exercising the one species of labour, impose the necessity of an apprenticeship, though with different degrees of rigour in different places. They leave the other free and open to every body. During the continuance of the apprenticeship, the whole labour of the apprentice belongs to his master. In the mean time he must, in many cases, be maintained by his parents or relations, and in almost all cases be cloathed by them. Some money too is commonly given to the master for teaching him his trade. They who cannot give money, give time, or become bound for more than the usual number of years; a consideration which, though it is not always advantageous to the master, on account of the usual idleness of apprentices, is always disadvantageous to the apprentice. In country labour, on the contrary, the labourer, while he is employed about the easier, learns the more difficult parts of his business, and his own labour maintains him through all the different stages of his employment. It is reasonable, therefore, that in Europe the wages of mechanics, artificers, and manufacturers, should be somewhat higher than those of common labourers. They are so accordingly and their superior gains make them in most places be considered as a superior rank of people. This superiority, however, is generally very small; the daily or weekly earnings of journeymen in the more common sorts of manufactures, such as those of plain linen and woollen cloth, computed at an average, are, in most places, very little more than the day wages of common labourers. Their employment, indeed, is more steady and uniform, and the superiority of their earnings, taking the whole year together, may be somewhat greater. It seems evidently, however, to be no greater than what is sufficient to compensate the superior expence of their education.

Education in the ingenious arts and in the liberal professions, is still more tedious and expensive. The pecuniary recompence, therefore, of painters and sculptors, of lawyers and physicians, ought to be much more liberal: and it is so accordingly.[2]

Thirdly, The wages of labour in different occupations vary with the constancy or inconstancy of employment.

Employment is much more constant in some trades than in others. In the greater part of manufactures, a journeyman may be pretty sure of employment almost every day in the year that he is able to work. A mason or bricklayer, on the contrary, can work neither in hard frost nor in foul weather, and his employment at all other times depends upon the occasional calls of his customers. He is liable, in consequence, to be frequently without any. What he earns, therefore, while he is employed, must not only maintain him while he is idle, but make him some compensation for those anxious and desponding moments which the thought of so precarious a situation must sometimes occasion.[3]

Fourthly, The wages of labour vary according to the small or great trust which must be reposed in the workmen.

The wages of goldsmiths and Jewellers are every-where superior to those of many other workmen, not only of equals but of much superior ingenuity; on account of the precious materials with which they are intrusted.

We trust our health to the physician; our fortune and sometimes our life and reputation to the lawyer and attorney. Such confidence could not safely be reposed in people of a very mean or low condition. Their reward must be such, therefore, as may give them that rank in society which so important a trust requires. The long time and the great expence which must be laid out in their education, when combined with this circumstance, necessarily enhance still further the price of their labour.[4]

Fifthly, The wages of labour in different employments vary according to the probability or improbability of success in them.

The probability that any particular person shall ever be qualified for the employment to which he is educated, is very different in different occupations. In the greater part of mechanic trades, success is almost certain; but very uncertain in the liberal professions. Put your son apprentice to a shoemaker, there is little doubt of his learning to make a pair of shoes: But send him to study the law, it is at least twenty to one if ever he makes such proficiency as will enable him to live by the business. In a perfectly fair lottery, those who draw the prizes ought to gain all that is lost by those who draw the blanks. In a profession where twenty fail for one that succeeds, that one ought to gain all that should have been gained by the unsuccessful twenty. The counsellor at law who, perhaps, at near forty years of age, begins to make something by his profession, ought to receive the retribution, not only of his own so tedious and expensive education, but of that of more than twenty others who are never likely to make any thing by it. How extravagant soever the fees of counsellors at law may sometimes appear, their real retribution is never equal to this. Compute in any particular place, what is likely to be annually gained, and what is likely to be annually spent, by all the different workmen in any common trade, such as that of shoemakers or weavers, and you will find that the former sum will generally exceed the latter. But make the same computation with regard to all the counsellors and students of law, in all the different inns of court, and you will find that their annual gains bear but a very small proportion to their annual expence, even though you rate the former as high, and the latter as low, as can well be done. The lottery of the law, therefore, is very far from being a perfectly fair lottery; and that, as well as many other liberal and honourable professions, is, in point of pecuniary gain, evidently under-recompenced.

Those professions keep their level, however, with other occupations, and, notwithstanding these discouragements, all the most generous and liberal spirits are eager to crowd into them. Two different causes contribute to recommend them. First, the desire of the reputation which attends upon superior excellence in any of them; and secondly, the natural confidence which every man has more or less, not only in his own abilities, but in his own good fortune.

To excel in any profession, in which but few arrive at mediocrity, is the most decisive mark of what is called genius or superior talents. The public admiration which attends upon such distinguished abilities, makes always a part of their reward; a greater or smaller in proportion as it is higher or lower in degree. It makes a considerable part of that reward in the profession of physic; a still greater perhaps in that of law; in poetry and philosophy it makes almost the whole.

There are some very agreeable and beautiful talents of which the possession commands a certain sort of admiration; but of which the exercise for the sake of gain is considered, whether from reason or prejudice, as a sort of public prostitution. The pecuniary recompence, therefore, of those who exercise them in this manner, must be sufficient, not only to pay for the time, labour, and expence of acquiring the talents, but for the discredit which attends the employment of them as the means of subsistence. The exorbitant rewards of players, opera-singers, opera-dancers &c. are founded upon those two principles; the rarity and beauty of the talents, and the discredit of employing them in this manner. It seems absurd at first sight that we should despise their persons and yet reward their talents with the most profuse liberality. While we do the one, however, we must of necessity do the other. Should the public opinion or prejudice ever alter with regard to such occupations, their pecuniary recompence would quickly diminish. More people would apply to them, and the competition would quickly reduce the price of their labour. Such talents, though far from being common, are by no means so rare as is imagined. Many people possess them in great perfection, who disdain to make this use of them; and many more are capable of acquiring them, if any thing could be made honourably by them.

The over-weening conceit, which the greater part of men have of their own abilities, is an ancient evil remarked by the philosophers and moralists of all ages. Their absurd presumption in their own good fortune, has been less taken notice of. It is, however, if possible, still more universal. There is no man living who, when in tolerable health and spirits, has not some share of it. The chance of gain is by every man more or less over-valued, and the chance of loss is by most men under-valued, and by scarce any man, who is in tolerable health and spirits, valued more than it is worth.

That the chance of gain is naturally over-valued, we may learn from the universal success of lotteries. The world neither ever saw, nor ever will see, a perfectly fair lottery; or one in which the whole gain compensated the whole loss; because the undertaker could make nothing by it. In the state lotteries the tickets are really not worth the price which is paid by the original subscribers, and yet commonly sell in the market for twenty, thirty, and sometimes forty per cent. advance. The vain hope of gaining some of the great prizes is the sole cause of this demand. The soberest people scarce look upon it as a folly to pay a small sum for the chance of gaining ten or twenty thousand pounds; though they know that even that small sum is perhaps twenty or thirty per cent. more than the chance is worth. In a lottery in which no prize exceeded twenty pounds, though in other respects it approached much nearer to a perfectly fair one than the common state lotteries, there would not be the same demand for tickets. In order to have a better chance for some of the great prizes, some people purchase several tickets, and others, small shares in a still greater number. There is not, however, a more certain proposition in mathemetics, than that the more tickets you adventure upon, the more likely you are to be a loser. Adventure upon all the tickets in the lottery, and you lose for certain; and the greater the number of your tickets the nearer you approach to this certainty.[5]

The contempt of risk and the presumptuous hope of success, are in no period of life more active than at the age at which young people chuse their professions. How little the fear of misfortune is then capable of balancing the hope of good luck, appears still more evidently in the readiness of the common people to enlist as soldiers, or to go to sea, than in the eagerness of those of better fashion to enter into what are called the liberal professions.[6]

## *INEQUALITIES DUE TO PUBLIC POLICY*

According to Smith, economic progress could best be realized where there was perfect liberty. This meant that people had the freedom to enter any business or occupation, that capital could be moved without artificial impediment, and that workers were free to travel to find jobs. These conditions did not always prevail in his time. Smith considered the public policies that denied freedom to be sources of unjustified income inequalities.

It does this chiefly in the three following ways. First, by restraining the competition in some employments to a smaller number than would otherwise be disposed to enter into them; secondly, by increasing it in others beyond what it naturally would be; and, thirdly, by obstructing the free circulation of labour and stock, both from employment to employment and from place to place.

First, The policy of Europe occasions a very important inequality in the whole of the advantages and disadvantages of the different employments of labour and stock, by restraining the competition in some employments to a smaller number than might otherwise be disposed to enter into them.

The exclusive privileges of corporations are the principal means it makes use of for this purpose.[7]

The exclusive privilege of an incorporated trade necessarily restrains the competition, in the town where it is established, to those who are free of the trade. To have served an apprenticeship in the town, under a master properly qualified, is commonly the necessary requisite for obtaining this freedom. The bye-laws of the corporation regulate sometimes the number of apprentices which any master is allowed to have, and almost always the number of years which each apprentice is obliged to serve. The intention of both regulations is to restrain the competition to a much smaller number than might otherwise be disposed to enter into the trade. The limitation of the number of apprentices restrains it directly. A long term of apprenticeship restrains it more indirectly, but as effectually, by increasing the expence of education.

In Sheffield no master cutler can have more than one apprentice at a time, by a bye-law of the corporation. In Norfolk and Norwich no master weaver can have more than two apprentices, under pain of forfeiting five pounds a month to the king. No master hatter can have more than two apprentites any-where in England, or in the English plantations, under pain of forfeiting five pounds a month, half to the king, and half to him who shall sue in any court of

record. Both these regulations, though they
have been confirmed by a public law of the
kingdom, are evidently dictated by the same
corporation spirit which enacted the bye-law
of Sheffield. The silk weavers in London had
scarce been incorporated a year when they
enacted a bye-law, restraining any master
from having more than two apprentices at
a time. It required a particular act of parliament to rescind this bye-law.[8]

These supply restrictions allowed members of
guilds to receive higher incomes than otherwise
would be the case. Perhaps more seriously, they had
the effect of depriving outsiders from earning a living in these occupations.

The property which every man has in his
own labour, as it is the original foundation
of all other property, so it is the most sacred
and inviolable. The patrimony of a poor man
lied in the strength and dexterity of his
hands; and to hinder him from employing
this strength and dexterity in what manner
he thinks proper without injury to his neighbour, is a plain violation of this most sacred
property. It is a manifest encroachment upon
the just liberty both of the workman, and of
those who might be disposed to employ him.
As it hinders the one from working at what
he thinks proper, so it hinders the others

from employing whom they think proper. To judge whether he is fit to be employed, may surely be trusted to the discretion of the employers whose interest it so much concerns. The affected anxiety of the law-giver lest they should employ an improper person, is evidently as impertinent as it is oppressive.[9]

Not only did long apprenticeships give little protection against bad work, but they also had a harmful effect on the work habits of the young.

The institution of long apprenticeships can give no security that insufficient workmanship shall not frequently be exposed to public sale. When this is done it is generally the effect of fraud, and not of inability; and the longest apprenticeship can give no security against fraud. Quite different regulations are necessary to prevent this abuse. The sterling mark upon plate, and the stamps upon linen and woollen cloth, give the purchasers much greater security than any statute of apprenticeship. He generally looks at these, but never thinks it worth while to enquire whether the workmen had served a seven years apprenticeship.

The institution of long apprenticeships has no tendency to form young people to industry. A journeyman who works by the piece is likely to be industrious, because he derives a benefit from every exertion of his industry. An apprentice is likely to be idle, and almost always is so because he has no immediate interest to be otherwise. In the inferior employments, the sweets of labour consist altogether in the recompence of labour. They who are soonest in a condition to enjoy the sweets of it, are likely soonest to conceive a relish for it, and to acquire the early habit of industry. A young man naturally conceives an aversion to labour, when for a long time he received no benefit from it. The boys who are put out apprentices from public charities are generally bound for more than the usual number of years, and they generally turn out very idle and worthless.[10]

All in all, it was a bad system in which the consumer was poorly served.

Long apprenticeships are altogether unnecessary. The arts, which are much superior to common trades, such as those of making clocks and watches, contain no such mystery as to require a long course of instruction. The first invention of such beautiful machines, indeed, and even that of some of the instruments employed in making them, must, no doubt, have been the work of deep thought and long time, and may justly be considered as among the happiest efforts of human ingenuity. But when both have been fairly invented and are well understood, to explain to any young man, in the completest manner, how to apply the instruments and how to construct the machines, cannot well require more than the lessons of a few weeks: perhaps those of a few days might be sufficient. In the common mechanic trades, those of a few days might certainly be sufficient. The dexterity of hand, indeed, even in common trades, cannot be acquired without much practice and experience. But a young man would practise with much more diligence and attention, if from the beginning he wrought as a journeyman, being paid in proportion to the little work which he could execute, and paying in his turn for the materials which he might sometimes spoil through awkwardness and inexperience. His education would generally in this way be more effectual, and always less tedious and expensive. The master, indeed, would be a loser. He would lose all the wages of the apprentice, which he now saves, for seven years together. In the end, perhaps, the apprentice himself would be a loser. In a trade so easily learnt he would have more competitors, and his wages, when he came to be a complete workman, would be much less than at present. The same increase of competition would reduce the profits of the masters as well as the wages of the workmen. The trades, the crafts, the mysteries, would all be losers. But the public would be a gainer, the work of all artificers coming in this way much cheaper to market.

It is to prevent this reduction of price, and consequently of wages and profit, by restraining that free competition which would most certainly occasion it, that all corporations, and the greater part of corporation laws, have been established.[11]

The pretence that corporations are necessary for the better government of the trade, is without any foundation. The real and effectual discipline which is exercised over a workman, is not that of his corporation, but that of his customers. It is the fear of losing their employment which restrains his frauds and corrects his negligence. An exclusive corporation necessarily weakens the force of this discipline. A particular set of workmen must then be employed, let them behave well or ill. It is upon this account, that in many large incorporated towns no tolerable workmen are to be found, even in some of the most necessary trades. If you would have your work tolerably executed, it must be done in the suburbs, where the workmen, having no exclusive privilege, have nothing but their character to depend upon, and you must then smuggle it into the town as well as you can.[12]

Interestingly, another passage in the same chapter reveals Smith's preference for country people.

The inhabitants of the country, dispersed in distant places, cannot easily combine together. They have not only never been incorporated, but the corporation spirit never has prevailed among them. No apprenticeship has ever been thought necessary to qualify for husbandry, the great trade of the country. After what are called the fine arts, and the liberal professions, however, there is perhaps no trade which requires so great a variety of knowledge and experience. The innumerable volumes which have been written upon it in all languages, may satisfy us, that among the wisest and most learned nations, it has never been regarded as a matter very easily understood. And from all those volumes we shall in vain attempt to collect that knowledge of its various and complicated operations, which is commonly possessed even by the common farmer; how contemptuously soever the very contemptible authors of some of them may sometimes affect to speak of him. There is scarce any common mechanic trade, on the contrary, of which all the operations may not be as completely and distinctly explained in a pamphlet of a very few pages, as it is possible for words illustrated by figures to explain them. In the history of the arts, now publishing by the French academy of sciences, several of them are actually explained in this manner. The direction of operations, besides, which must be varied with every change of the weather, as well as with many other accidents, requires much more judgment and discretion, than that of those which are always the same or very nearly the same.

Not only the art of the farmer, the general direction of the operations of husbandry, but many inferior branches of country labour, require much more skill and experience than the greater part of mechanic trades. The man who works upon brass and iron, works with instruments and upon materials of which the temper is always the same, or very nearly the same. But the man who ploughs the ground with a team of horses or oxen, works with instruments of which the health, strength, and temper, are very different upon different occasions. The condition of the materials which he works upon too is as variable as that of the instruments which he works with, and both require to

be managed with much judgment and discretion. The common ploughman, though
generally regarded as the pattern of stupidity and ignorance, is seldom defective in this
judgment and discretion. He is less accustomed, indeed, to social intercourse than the
mechanic who lives in a town. His voice and
language are more uncouth and more difficult to be understood by those who are not
used to them. His understanding, however,
being accustomed to consider a greater variety of objects, is generally much superior
to that of the other, whose whole attention
from morning till night is commonly occu-
pied in performing one or two very simple
operations. How much the lower ranks of
people in the country are really superior to
those of the town, is well known to every
man whom either business or curiosity has
led to converse much with both.[13]

The policy of subsidization was another source of
inequality. Here, however, the effect was to lower
the wage.

Secondly, The policy of Europe, by increasing the competition in some employments
beyond what it naturally would be, occasions another inequality of an opposite kind
in the whole of the advantages and disadvantages of the different employments of

labour and stock.

It has been considered as of so much importance that a proper number of young people should be educated for certain professions, that, sometimes the public, and sometimes the piety of private founders have established many pensions, scholarships, exhibitions, bursaries, &c. for this purpose, which draw many more people into those trades than could otherwise pretend to follow them. In all christian countries, I believe, the education of the greater part of churchmen is paid for in this manner. Very few of them are educated altogether at their own expence. The long, tedious, and expensive education, therefore, of those who are, will not always procure them a suitable reward, the church being crowded with people who, in order to get employment, are willing to accept of a much smaller recompence than what such an education would otherwise have entitled them to; and in this manner the competition of the poor takes away the reward of the rich.[14]

In professions in which there are no benefices, such as law and physic, if an equal proportion of people were educated at the public expence, the competition would soon be so great, as to sink very much their pecuniary reward. It might then not be worth any man's while to educate his son to either of those professions at his own expence. They would be entirely abandoned to such as had been educated by those public charities, whose numbers and necessities would oblige them in general to content themselves with a very miserable recompence, to the entire degredation of the now respectable professions of law and physic.

That unprosperous race of men commonly called men of letters, are pretty much in the situation which lawyers and physicians probably would be in upon the foregoing supposition. In every part of Europe the greater part of them have been educated for the church, but have been hindered by different reasons from entering into holy orders. They have generally, therefore, been educated at the public expence, and their numbers are every-where so great as commonly to reduce the price of their labour to a very paultry recompence.

Before the invention of the art of printing, the only employment by which a man of letters could make any thing by his talents, was that of a public or private teacher, or by communicating to other people the curious and useful knowledge which he had acquired himself: And this is still surely a more honourable, a more useful, and in general even a more profitable employment than that of writing for a book seller, to which the art of printing has given occasion. The time and study, the genius, knowledge, and application requisite to qualify an eminent teacher of the sciences, are at least equal to what is necessary for the greatest practitioners in law and physic. But the usual reward of the eminent teacher bears no proportion to that of the lawyer or physician; because the trade of the one is crowded with indigent people who have been brought up to it at the public expence; whereas those of the other two are incumbered with very few who have not been educated at their own. The usual recompence, however, of public and private teachers, small as it may appear, would undoubtedly be less than it is, if the competition of those yet more indigent men of letters who write for bread was not taken out of the market. Before the invention of the art of printing, a scholar and a beggar seem to have been terms very nearly synonymous. The different governors of the universities before that time appear to have often granted licences to their scholars to beg.[15]

This policy, however, did have a beneficial social effect.

This inequality is upon the whole, perhaps, rather advantageous than hurtful to the public. It may somewhat degrade the profession of a public teacher; but the cheapness of literary education is surely an advantage which greatly over-balances this trifling inconveniency. The public too might derive still greater benefit from it, if the constitution of those schools and colleges, in which education is carried on was more reasonable than it is at present through the greater part of Europe.[16]

Smith then discussed the policies which restricted the mobility of labor and capital.

Thirdly, The policy of Europe, by obstructing the free circulation of labour and stock both from employment to employment, and from place to place, occasions in some cases a very inconvenient inequality in the whole of the advantages and disadvantages of their different employments.

The statute of apprenticeship obstructs the free circulation of labour from one employment to another, even in the same place. The exclusive privileges of corporations obstruct it from one place to another, even in the same employment.

It frequently happens that while high wages are given to the workmen in one manufacture, those in another are obliged to content themselves with bare subsistence. The one is in an

advancing state, and has, therefore, a continual demand for new hands: The other is
in a declining state, and the super-abun-
dance of hands is continually increasing.
Those two manufactures may sometimes be
in the same town, and sometimes in the
same neighbourhood, without being able to
lend the least assistance to one another. The
statute of apprenticeship may oppose it in
the one case, and both that and an exclusive
corporation in the other. In many different
manufactures, however, the operations are
so much alike, that the workmen could easily change trades with one another, if those
absurd laws did not hinder them.[17]

Whatever obstructs the free circulation of
labour from one employment to another, obstructs that of stock likewise; the quantity of
stock which can be employed in any branch
of business depending very much upon that
of the labour which can be employed in it.
Corporation laws, however, give less obstruction to the free circulation of stock from one
place to another than to that of labour. It is
everywhere much easier for a wealthy merchant to obtain the privilege of trading in a
town corporate, than for a poor artificer to
obtain that of working in it.[18]

Those poor laws that restrict the mobility of labor were especially harmful to the common worker.

The very unequal price of labour which we frequently find in England in places at no great distance from one another, is probably owing to the obstruction which the law of settlements gives to a poor man who would carry his industry from one parish to another without a certificate. A single man, indeed, who is healthy and industrious, may sometimes reside by sufferance without one; but a man with a wife and family who should attempt to do so, would in most parishes be sure of being removed, and if the single man should afterwards marry, he would generally be removed likewise. The scarcity of hands in one parish, therefore, cannot always be relieved by their superabundance in another, as it is constantly in Scotland, and, I believe, in all other countries where there is no difficulty of settlement. In such countries, though wages may sometimes rise a little in the neighbourhood of a great town, or wherever else there is an extraordinary demand for labour, and sink gradually as the distance from such places increases, till they fall back to the common rate of the country; yet we never meet with those sudden and unaccountable differences in the wages of neighbouring places which we sometimes find in England, where it is often more difficult for a poor man to pass the artificial boundary of a parish, than an arm of the sea or a ridge of high mountains, natural boundaries which sometimes separate very distinctly different rates of wages in other countries.

To remove a man who has committed no misdemeanour from the parish where he chuses to reside, is an evident violation of natural liberty and justice. The common people of England, however, so jealous of their liberty, but like the common people of most other countries never rightly understanding wherein it consists, have now for more than a century together suffered themselves to be exposed to this oppression without a remedy. Though men of reflection too have sometimes complained of the law of settlements as a public grievance; yet it has never been the object of any general popular clamour, such as that against general warrants, an abusive practice undoubtedly, but such a one as was not likely to occasion any general oppression. There is scarce a poor man in England of forty years of age, I will venture to say, who has not in some part of his life felt himself most cruelly oppressed by this ill-contrived law of settlements.[19]

# THE CONSUMER ADVOCATE

We already have seen how Smith gave his support to high wages. The passage below, surely, would warm the cockles of any trade unionist's heart.

What are the common wages of labour, depends every where upon the contract usually made between those two parties, whose interests are by no means the same. The workmen desire to get as much, the masters to give as little as possible. The former are disposed to combine in order to raise, the latter in order to lower the wages of labour. It is not, however, difficult to foresee which of the two parties, must upon all ordinary occasions, have the advantage in the dispute, and force the other into a compliance with their terms. The masters, being fewer in number, can combine much more easily; and the law, besides, authorises, or at least does not prohibit their combinations, while it prohibits those of the workmen. We have no acts of parliament against combining to lower the price of work; but many against combining to raise it. In all such disputes the masters can hold out much longer. A landlord, a farmer, a master manufacturer, or merchant, though they did not employ a single workman, could generally live a year or two upon the stocks which they have already acquired.

Many workmen could not subsist a week, few could subsist a month, and scarce any a year without employment. In the long-run the workman may be as necessary to his master as his master is to him, but the necessity is not so immediate.

We rarely hear, it has been said, of the combinations of masters, though frequently of those of workmen. But whoever imagines, upon this account, that masters rarely combine, is as ignorant of the world as of the subject. Masters are always and every where in a sort of tacit, but constant and uniform combination, not to raise the wages of labour above their actual rate. To violate this combination is every where a most unpopular action, and a sort of reproach to a master among his neighbours and equals. We seldom, indeed, hear of this combination, because it is the usual, and one may say, the natural state of things which nobody ever bears of. Masters too sometimes enter into particular combinations to sink the wages of labour even below this rate. These are always conducted with the utmost silence and secrecy, till the moment of execution, and when the workmen yield, as they sometimes do, without resistance, though severely felt by them, they are never heard of by other people. Such combinations, however, are frequently resisted by a contrary defensive

combination of the workmen; who sometimes too, without any provocation of this
kind, combine of their own accord to raise
the price of their labour. Their usual pre-
tences are, sometimes the high price of provisions; sometimes the great profit which
their masters make by their work. But
whether their combinations be offensive or
defensive, they are always abundantly
heard of. In order to bring the point to a
speedy decision, they have always recourse
to the loudest clamour, and sometimes to
the most shocking violence and outrage.
They are desperate, and act with the folly
and extravagance of desperate men, who
must either starve, or frighten their masters
into an immediate compliance with their de-
mands. The masters upon these occasions
are just as clamorous upon the other side,
and never cease to call aloud for the assistance of the civil magistrate, and the rigorous execution of those laws which have been
enacted with so much severity against the
combinations of servants, labourers, and
journeymen. The workmen, accordingly,
very seldom derive any advantage from the
violence of those tumultuous combinations,
which, partly from the interposition of the
civil magistrate, partly from the superior
steadiness of the masters, partly from the
necessity which the greater part of the

workmen are under of submitting for the sake of present subsistence, generally end in nothing, but the punishment or ruin of the ringleaders.[20]

Smith even advanced a personnel policy, the ingredients of which were high wages and a moderate work schedule.

The liberal reward of labour, as it encourages the propagation, so it increases the industry of the common people. The wages of labour are the encouragement of industry, which, like every other human quality, improves in proportion to the encouragement it receives. A plentiful subsistence increases the bodily strength of the labourer, and the comfortable hope of bettering his condition, and of ending his days perhaps in ease and plenty, animates him to exert that strength to the utmost. Where wages are high, accordingly, we shall always find the workmen more active, diligent, and expeditious, than where they are low; in England, for example, than in Scotland; in the neighbourhood of great towns, than in remote country places. Some workmen, indeed, when they can earn in four days what will maintain them through the week, will be idle the other three. This, however, is by no means the case with the greater part. Workmen,

on the contrary, when they are liberally paid
by the piece, are very apt to over-work
themselves, and to ruin their health and
constitution in a few years. A carpenter in
London, and in some other places, is not
supposed to last in his utmost vigour above
eight years. Something of the same kind
happens in many other trades, in which the
workmen are paid by the piece; as they generally are in manufactures, and even in
country labour, wherever wages are higher
than ordinary. Almost every class of artificers is subject to some peculiar infirmity occasioned by excessive application to their
peculiar species of work. Ramuzzini, an eminent Italian physician, has written a particular book concerning such diseases. We
do not reckon our soldiers the most industrious set of people among us. Yet when soldiers have been employed in some
particular sorts of work, and liberally paid
by the piece, their officers have frequently
been obliged to stipulate with the undertaker, that they should not be allowed to
earn above a certain sum every day, according to the rate at which they were paid. Till
this stipulation was made, mutual emulation and the desire of greater gain, frequently prompted them to over-work
themselves, and to hurt their health by excessive labour. Excessive application during

four days of the week, is frequently the real cause of the idleness of the other three, so much and so loudly complained of. Great labour, either of mind or body, continued for several days together, is in most men naturally followed by a great desire of relaxation, which, if not restrained by force or by some strong necessity, is almost irresistible. It is the call of nature, which requires to be relieved by some indulgence, sometimes of ease only, but sometimes too of dissipation and diversion. If it is not complied with, the consequences are often dangerous, and sometimes fatal, and such as almost always, sooner or later, bring on the peculiar infirmity of the trade. If masters would always listen to the dictates of reason and humanity, they have frequently occasion rather to moderate, than to animate the application of many of their workmen. It will be found, I believe, in every sort of trade, that the man who works so moderately, as to be able to work constantly, not only preserves his health the longest, but, in the course of the year, executes the greatest quantity of work.[21]

The words below should confirm that his sympathies did not lie with the employer.

Our merchants and master-manufacturers complain much of the bad effects of high wages in raising the price, and thereby lessening the sale of their goods both at home and abroad. They say nothing concerning the bad effects of high profits. They are silent with regard to the pernicious effects of their own gains. They complain only of those of other people.[22]

People of the same trade seldom meet together even for merriment and diversion, but the conversation ends in a conspiracy against the public, or in some contrivance to raise prices.[23]

The interest of the dealers, however, in any particular branch of trade or manufactures, is always in some respects different from, and even opposite to, that of the public. To widen the market and to narrow the competition, is always the interest of the dealers. To widen the market may frequently be agreeable enough to the interest of the public; but to narrow the competition must always be against it, and can serve only to enable the dealers, by raising their profits above what they naturally would be, to levy, for their own benefit, an absurd tax upon the rest of their fellow-citizens. The proposal of any new law or regulation of commerce which comes from this order, ought always to be listened to with great precaution, and ought never to be adopted till after having been long and carefully examined, not only with the most scrupulous, but with the most suspicious attention. It comes from an order of men, whose interest is never exactly the same with that of the public, who have generally an interest to deceive and even to oppress the public, and who accordingly have, upon many occasions, both deceived and oppressed it.[24]

It is the industry which is carried on for the benefit of the rich and the powerful, that is principally encouraged by our mercantile system. That which is carried on for the benefit of the poor and the indigent, is too often, either neglected, or oppressed.[25]

Smith attacked monopolistic practices wherever he saw them and was not really the defender of any one social class. Rather, he sought to explain how to achieve economic progress in which all would share. He truly was an advocate for the consumer.

Consumption is the sole end and purpose of all production; and the interest of the producer ought to be attended to, only so far as it may be necessary for promoting that of the consumer. The maxim is so perfectly self-evident, that it would be absurd to attempt to prove it. But in the mercantile system, the interest of the consumer is almost constantly sacrificed to that of the producer; and it seems to consider production,and not consumption, as the ultimate end and object of all industry and commerce.[26]

Although Smith's main concern was not with income differentials, it easily can be implied that his system of natural liberty would not only provide more output, but would also lead to greater equality. He believed that humans are quite similar at birth and that environmental conditions play an important role in the development of their talents and the economic success they enjoy.

The difference of natural talents in different men is, in reality, much less than we are aware of; and the very different genius which appears to distinguish men of different professions, when grown up to maturity, is not upon many occasions so much the cause, as the effect of the division of labour. The difference between the most dissimilar characters, between a philosopher and a common street porter, for example, seems to arise not so much from nature, as from habit, custom, and education. When they came into the world, and for the first six or eight years of their existence, they were perhaps, very much alike, and neither their parents nor playfellows could perceive any remarkable difference. About that age, or soon after, they come to be employed in very different occupations. The difference of talents comes then to be taken notice of, and widens by degrees, till at last the vanity of the philosopher is willing to acknowledge scarce any resemblance.[27]

By nature a philosopher is not in genius and disposition half so different from a street porter, as a mastiff is from a greyhound, or a greyhound from a spaniel, or this last from a shepherd's dog.[28]

The removal of the monopolistic and artificial restrictions of mercantilism would extend opportunity throughout society. Human talents would be given a better chance to develop and a more equal distribution of income would result.

# CHAPTER 9

## THE LEGACY of ADAM SMITH

The publication of *The Wealth of Nations* was an immediate success. The book went through four editions in Smith's lifetime, was translated into several languages, and made its author famous. The insights developed in this work, along with its elegant prose, allowed it wide distribution. It found its way into the libraries of the intelligentsia as well as statesmen including the Americans Thomas Jefferson, Alexander Hamilton and John Adams.

Lord North employed some of Smith's tax proposals in constructing his 1777 and 1778 budget. Also, Smith was consulted by government officials about British policy toward the American colonies and Ireland. He first was quoted in Parliament in 1783 by the Whig leader, Charles Fox, and in later years by several others including the son of the Earl of Chatham, William Pitt the younger. This man who served as Prime Minister for eighteen years and who worked diligently to implement Smith's ideas, particularly those on tariffs, taxes, and government borrowing, had this to say while introducing the 1792 budget:

> Simple and obvious as this principle is, and felt and observed as it must have been in a greater or less degree, even from the

earliest periods, I doubt whether it has ever been fully developed and sufficiently explained, but in the writings of an author of our own times, now unfortunately no more. (I mean the author of a celebrated treatise on The Wealth of Nations), whose extensive knowledge of detail, and depth of philosophical research will, I believe, furnish the best solution to every question connected with the history of commerce, or with the systems of political economy.[1]

In 1778, Smith was made a Commissioner of Customs in Scotland. This position paid him the annual sum of six hundred pounds, which when joined with his pension from tutoring, and royalties from his publications, afforded him a very comfortable living. He continued to read fine literature, maintained his club memberships, and enjoyed stimulating conversation with the numerous friends that he invited to his home. The University of Glasgow awarded him the honorary position of Rector in 1787. He maintained reasonably good health and good spirits for the next few years, but, finally, this kind man, much beloved by his students and friends, died at age sixty-seven on July 17, 1790.

*The Wealth of Nations* was not a perfect book. For instance, Smith's theory of value was incomplete, his notion of capital not always clear, and anyone who has watched television programs on nature is aware that animals do cooperate with each other. Moreover, we know that not all in this work was original with Smith. What then were his contributions?

The systematic study of economics was in its infancy during the time of Adam Smith. His genius was his ability to organize and interpret information and ideas and to present them differently and in a more unified manner than had his predecessors. The catholicity of his thought is indicated by his analysis of all the vital sectors of the economy. *The Wealth of Nations* became the starting point for subsequent generations of economic scholarship.

Adam Smith's precepts on economic freedom were not quickly adopted because the defenders of monopolistic privilege were deeply entrenched. It was not until the 1840s that England embraced free trade. American industry was kept under varying degrees of tariff protection throughout the nineteenth century. In economics, however, things seldom are all or nothing and the nations which generally have followed his advice have been handsomely rewarded. In other words, Smith's system has passed the ultimate test of economic theory — it worked. Moreover, it has worked over a long period of time.

Smith's focus was upon the individual and he was aware that there were many dimensions to human behavior. of course, the economic side dominates *The Wealth of Nations* and although evidence of this already has been presented, it is worthwhile to offer just a few more quotations.

. . . landlords, like all other men, love to reap where they never sowed.[2]

With the greater part of rich people, the chief enjoyment of riches consists in the parade of riches, which in their eye is never so complete as when they appear to possess those decisive marks of opulence which nobody can possess but themselves. In their eyes the merit of an object which is in any degree either useful or beautiful, is greatly enhanced by its scarcity, or by the great labour which it requires to collect any considerable quantity of it, a labour which nobody can afford to pay but themselves. Such objects they are willing to purchase at a higher price than things much more beautiful and useful, but more common.[3]

The pride of man makes him love to domineer, and nothing mortifies him so much as to be obliged to condescend to persuade his inferiors.[4]

All for ourselves, and nothing for other people, seems, in every age of the world, to have been the vile maxim of the masters of mankind.[5]

However, we must not forget what Smith said in *The Theory of Moral Sentiments*. In this earlier work, he not only explained how one's conscience kept self-interest in check but also that human behavior often reflected such virtues as kindness and generosity. Man, after all, is not consistently selfish.

> How selfish soever man may be supposed, there are evidently some principles in his nature, which interest him in the fortune of others and render their happiness necessary to him, though he derives nothing from it except the pleasure of seeing it.[6]

*The Theory of Moral Sentiments* and *The Wealth of Nations* are best understood as complementary rather than contradictory works. The former not only showed the self-interest of man restrained by an "impartial spectator" but also endowed him with positive "social passions." In the latter work, self-interest is harnessed by competition. Now self-interest may not be the loftiest motive, but Smith considered it to be one of the most powerful. In other words, Smith was very much aware of the different dimensions of human behavior. He tried to portray man as he is and did not attempt to present him in some ideal form or with the potential for perfection in this world.

Smith's was a formula for long-run success that was independent of whoever happened to be holding political office. The incentives of reward and punishment that it contained meant that you did not need to elect "good people" for it to work. Adam

Smith believed that both individuals and nations would prosper where people were not impeded by artificial obstacles and were free to exercise their initiative. Free competitive markets would insure that business produced what consumers valued the most in a world of scarcity. This system would see to it that prices reflected costs and it also would generate a more equitable distribution of income as real economic growth worked its way throughout society. This eighteenth-century consumer advocate was so radical as to believe that economic liberty not only would promote a generally higher standard of living but also would provide greater equality.

The basic problem to which Smith addressed himself has always been and always will be with us — how are the scarce resources of land, capital and labor best allocated among competing uses. Rather than deferring to some elite group, Smith placed his trust in the people. They should make the decisions and they should and would receive the rewards.

# NOTES
## CHAPTER 1

1. Adam Smith, *An Inquiry Into The Nature And Causes of The Wealth of Nations*, ed. with an introduction by Edwin Cannan and an introduction by Max Lerner (New York: The Modern Library, Random House, Inc. 1937).

## CHAPTER 2

1. Among these are gross national product, per capita income, and the unemployment rate.

2. *An Essay on Trade and Commerce* (London: Hooper, 1770) pp. 266-267, quoted in Wesley C. Mitchell, *Types of Economic Theory*, 2 Vol. ed. and with an introduction by Joseph Dorfman (New York: Augustus M. Kelley Publishers, 1967), I, p. 115.

3. Young, *The Farmer's Tour Through the East of England*, 4 vols. (London: Strahan, 1771), II, p. 361, quoted in Wesley C. Mitchell, *Types of Economic Theory*, p. 115.

## CHAPTER 3

1. Adam Smith, *The Theory of Moral Sentiments*, ed. by D. D. Raphael and A. L. Macfie (Indianapolis: Liberty Classics, 1982), p. 137.

2. Wesley C. Mitchell, *Types of Economic Theory*, 2 Vol. ed. and with an introduction by Joseph Dorfman (New York: Augustus M. Kelly Publishers, 1967), I, p. 118.

3. *Ibid.*, pp. 66-76.

# CHAPTER 4

1. Smith, *The Wealth of Nations*, p. LX.

2. *Ibid.*, p. 280.

3. *Ibid.*, p. 406.

4. *Ibid.*, p. 409.

5. *Ibid.*, p. 13.

6. *Ibid.*, p. 13.

7. *Ibid.*, p. 13, 14.

8. *Ibid.*, pp. 342-343.

9. *Ibid.*, pp. 744-745.

10. *Ibid.*, p. 61.

11. *Ibid.*, p. 147.

12. *Ibid.*, p. 3.

13. *Ibid.*, pp. 4-5.

14. *Ibid.*, pp. 7-9.

15. *Ibid.*, p. 17.

16. *Ibid.*, p. 416.

17. *Ibid.*, P. 13.

18. *Ibid.*, P. 321.

19. *Ibid.*, P. 321.

20. *Ibid.*, pp. 11-12.

21. *Ibid.*, p. 11.

22. *Ibid.*, pp. 330-331.

23. *Ibid.*, p. 69.

24. *Ibid.*, p. 81.

25. *Ibid.*, p. 79.

# CHAPTER 5

1. Smith, *The Wealth of Nations*, pp. 420-421.

2. *Ibid.*, pp. 423-424.

3. *Ibid.*, pp. 425-426.

4. *Ibid.*, pp. 429-430.

5. *Ibid.*, pp. 431-432.

6. *Ibid.*, p. 434.

7. *Ibid.*, p. 435.

8. *Ibid.*, pp. 435-436.

9. *Ibid.*, pp. 436-437.

10. *Ibid.*, pp. 437-439.

11. *Ibid.*, pp. 459-460.

12. *Ibid.*, pp. 472-473.

13. *Ibid.*, p. 475.

14. *Ibid.*, pp. 488-489.

15. *Ibid.*, p. 511.

16. *Ibid.*, p. 618.

17. *Ibid.*, p. 421.

18. *Ibid.*, p. 423.

19. *Ibid.*, pp. 460-462.

20. *Ibid.*, pp. 463-464.

# CHAPTER 6

1. Smith, *The Wealth of Nations*, p. 423.

2. *Ibid.*, p. 605

3. *Ibid.*, p. 612.

4. *Ibid.*, pp. 614-615.

5. *Ibid.*, pp. 492-494.

6. *Ibid.*, p. 507.

7. *Ibid.*, pp. 325-326.

8. *Ibid.*, pp. 328-329.

9. *Ibid.*, p. 555.

10. *Ibid.*, pp. 570-572.

11. *Ibid.*, pp. 579-580.

12. *Ibid.*, p. 626.

13. *Ibid.*, pp. 587-588.

14. *Ibid.*, pp. 581-582.

15. *Ibid.*, pp. 589-590.

16. *Ibid.*, pp. 899-900.

# CHAPTER 7

1. Smith, *The Wealth of Nations*, p. 651.

2. *Ibid.*, p. 653.

3. *Ibid.*, pp. 659-660.

4. *Ibid.*, pp. 667-669.

5. *Ibid.*, pp. 669-670.

6. *Ibid.*, p. 681.

7. *Ibid.*, p. 681.

8. *Ibid.*, p. 689.

9. *Ibid.*, pp. 734-735.

10. *Ibid.*, pp. 739-740.

11. *Ibid.*, pp. 736-738.

12. *Ibid.*, pp. 717-721.

13. *Ibid.*, p. 728.

14. *Ibid.*, p. 777.

15. *Ibid.*, p. 778.

16. *Ibid.*, pp. 778-779.

17. *Ibid.*, p. 813.

18. *Ibid.*, pp. 832-833.

19. *Ibid.*, p. 849.

20. *Ibid.*, pp. 862-863.

21. *Ibid.*, p. 863.

22. *Ibid.*, pp. 867-868.

23. *Ibid.*, p. 878.

24. *Ibid.*, p. 879.

25. *Ibid.*, pp. 882-883.

# CHAPTER 8

1. Smith, *The Wealth of Nations*, p. 100.

2. *Ibid.*, pp. 101-102.

3. *Ibid.*, p. 103.

4. *Ibid.*, p. 105.

5. *Ibid.*, pp. 106-108.

6. *Ibid.*, p. 109.

7. Smith uses the word corporation to refer to a craft guild. It does not have the meaning which we attach to it today.

8. *Ibid.*, pp. 118-119.

9. *Ibid.*, pp. 121-122.

10. *Ibid.*, p. 122.

11. *Ibid.*, p. 123.

12. *Ibid.*, p. 129.

13. *Ibid.*, pp. 126-127.

14. *Ibid.*, pp. 129-130.

15. *Ibid.*, pp. 131-132.

16. *Ibid.*, p. 134.

17. *Ibid.*, pp. 134-135.

18. *Ibid.*, p. 135.

19. *Ibid.*, pp. 140-141.

20. *Ibid.*, pp. 66-67.

21. *Ibid.*, pp. 81-82.

22. *Ibid.*, P. 98.

23. *Ibid.*, p. 128.

24. *Ibid.*, p. 250.

25. *Ibid.*, p. 609.

26. *Ibid.*, P. 625.

27. *Ibid.*, pp. 15-16.

28. *Ibid.*, p. 16.

# CHAPTER 9

1. Mitchell, *Types of Economic Theory*, p. 156.
2. Smith, *The Wealth of Nations*, p. 49.
3. *Ibid.*, p. 172.
4. *Ibid.*, p. 365.
5. *Ibid.*, pp. 388-389.
6. Smith, *The Theory of Moral Sentiments*, p. 9.

# SELECTED BIBLIOGRAPHY

1. Heckscher, Eli F. *Mercantilism,* revised edition edited by E. F. Soderlund, vol. 2. New York: The Macmillan Company, 1955.

2. Mitchell, Wesley C. *Types of Economic Theory,* edited and with an introduction by Joseph Dorfman, vols. 1 and 2. New York: Augustus M. Kelley, Publishers, 1967.

3. Rae, John. *Life of Adam Smith,* with an introduction by Jacob Viner. Fairfield, New Jersey: Augustus M. Kelley, Publishers, 1977.

4. Smith, Adam. *An Inquiry In to The Nature And Causes of The Wealth of Nations,* edited with an introduction by Edwin Cannan and an introduction by Max Lerner. New York: The Modern Library — Random House, Inc., 1937.

5. Smith, Adam. *The Theory of Moral Sentiments,* edited by D. D. Raphael and A. L. Macfie. Indianapolis: Liberty Classics, 1967.

# INDEX

Adams, John, 205

Addison, Joseph, 21

agriculture, 10, 18, 19, 20, 23, 121

America, 43, 54, 105, 110, 111, 112, 115, 116, 205, 207

apprenticeship, 19, 168, 171, 178-182, 184

Bengal, 97

Boswell, James, 3, 17, 21

bounty, 67, 77-81, 107 (see also subsidy)

Brazil, 105

capital, 30, 44-48, 58-60, 70, 73, 78, 79, 84, 89, 91,101-103, 105, 108, 119, 157, 160, 163, 167, 177, 190

colonies, 5, 7, 9, 23, 91, 104-118

competition, 2, 23, 26, 29-31, 35, 48, 73, 82, 85, 87, 88, 119, 140, 174, 177, 178, 182, 183, 186, 187, 189-191, 201, 209, 210

conscience, 17, 209

consumer, 2, 23, 36, 92, 100, 110-112, 181, 183, 195, 202, 203, 210

corporation, 70, 177-179, 183, 184, 192 (see also trade-guild)

Defoe, Daniel, 21

division of labor, 36-44, 51, 52, 74, 133, 203

Duke of Buccleuch, 18

Dutch, 161

duties and prohibitions, 7, 57, 62, 63, 65-67, 76, 82, 87, 92, 155, 156, 205, 207

East India Company, 8, 91, 97

economics-economy, 1, 3, 5, 6, 9, 15, 16, 18-20, 26, 83, 96, 105, 206, 207

economic growth, 2, 13, 18, 23, 26, 36, 45, 48-56, 100, 116, 133, 165, 177, 202, 210

Edinburgh, 15, 21

education, 133-152, 167-169, 171, 172, 182, 183, 188-190

England, 5, 8, 9, 11, 12, 19, 20, 33, 54, 103, 104, 109, 139, 141, 149, 150, 178, 192, 193, 198, 207

Europe, 5, 43, 67, 75, 86, 87, 90, 96, 104, 105, 112, 158, 159, 168, 169, 177, 186, 188, 190

Fielding, Henry, 21

Fox, Charles, 205

France, 8, 9, 18, 21, 54, 75-77, 106, 132, 144, 185

freedom, 3, 20, 57, 68, 75, 89, 90, 95-98, 108, 114, 135, 140, 145, 177, 178, 183, 191, 207, 210

Gainsborough, Thomas, 20

Glasgow University, 15, 18, 21, 206

government, 1, 2, 6, 7, 9, 12, 18, 23, 33, 91-164, 183, 205

Great Britain, 57, 58, 62-64, 70, 71, 76, 77, 87, 91, 105, 106, 108, 111-114, 116-118, 132, 155, 161, 162, 205

Greece, 114

Guinea, 76

Hamilton, Alexander, 205

Handel, George, 20

harmony of interests, 17, 57, 84-90

# Index

prices, 2, 8, 28-30, 34, 60, 78-80, 82, 98, 110, 188, 192, 195, 197, 201, 208, 210

productivity, 36-44

profits, 12, 28, 29, 34, 45, 48, 78, 79, 88, 98, 99, 108, 110, 113, 118, 120, 131, 167, 183, 197, 201

property, 20, 127-129, 158, 179

Protestant, 8, 11

public works-institutions, 130-151

Quakers, 34, 105

regulation, 8, 13, 30, 59, 72, 73, 92-95, 100, 108, 110, 145, 146, 178-180, 201

religion, 31-33, 100, 104, 105

rent, 28

Reynolds, Joshua, 20

Richardson, Samuel, 21

Roman Catholic Church, 11

Russia, 123

Scotland, 61, 138, 192, 198, 206

self-interest, 17, 26-29, 84, 85, 100, 102, 103, 209

Shakespeare, 3

Smith, Adam, 1-3, 13, 15-21, 23, 24, 26, 28, 30, 31, 34, 36, 42-45, 48, 51, 57, 62, 67, 71, 74, 79, 80, 83-85, 89, 91, 96, 100, 104, 109, 111, 112, 114, 116, 119, 120, 122, 127, 129, 136, 150, 152, 155, 158-161, 165, 177, 184, 195, 202, 203, 205, 210

sovereign, duties of, 119-151

Spain, 75, 106

state, 8, 9, 73, 96, 119, 121, 122, 127, 131, 135, 143, 152, 158, 163, 178

statesman, 66, 91, 109, 112

statutes of apprenticeship, 9, 70, 145, 190, 191

Steele, Richard, 21

subsidies, 7, 8, 80, 186 (see also bounty)

Swift, Dr., 155

taxes, 3, 9, 12, 23, 30, 64, 66, 80, 81, 114-117, 119, 131, 132, 152-157, 159, 201, 205

teacher, 32, 138-150, 188-190

Temple, William, 10

Theory of Moral Sentiments, The, 16-18, 208, 209

Townshend, Charles, 17, 18

trade-guild, 10, 19, 71, 78, 79, 98, 122, 137-139, 168, 171, 178, 179, 181-184, 187, 191, 199, 200, 201 (see also corporation)

trade union v. masters, 195-198

treaty, 81, 82, 114

Voltaire, 18

wages, 2, 8-10, 13, 19, 24, 34, 47, 48, 54, 55, 69, 165-176, 182, 183, 186, 190, 192, 193, 195, 196, 198, 199, 201

wealth, 6, 12, 23, 24, 43, 47, 54, 72, 81, 87-89, 102, 113, 116, 121

Wealth of Nations, The, 1-3, 16-18, 23, 24, 36, 117, 205, 206, 207, 209

West Indian, 110

Young, Arthur, 10